D1401468

MODERN WORLD NATIONS

MODERN WORLD NATIONS

Republic of Georgia

Zoran Pavlović
and
Charles F. Gritzner
South Dakota State University

Chelsea House Publishers
Philadelphia

Frontispiece: Flag of the Republic of Georgia

Cover: Tsminda Sameda church in the Caucasus Mountains, Georgia.

CHELSEA HOUSE PUBLISHERS

EDITOR IN CHIEF Sally Cheney
DIRECTOR OF PRODUCTION Kim Shinners
CREATIVE MANAGER Takeshi Takahashi
MANUFACTURING MANAGER Diann Grasse

Staff for REPUBLIC OF GEORGIA

EDITOR Lee Marcott
PRODUCTION ASSISTANT Jaimie Winkler
PICTURE RESEARCH 21st Century Publishing and Communications, Inc.
COVER AND SERIES DESIGNER Takeshi Takahashi
LAYOUT 21st Century Publishing and Communications, Inc.

http://www.chelseahouse.com

First Printing

1 3 5 7 9 8 6 4 2

Library of Congress Cataloging-in-Publication Data

Pavlovic, Zoran.
  Republic of Georgia / by Zoran Pavlovic and Charles Gritzner.
    p. cm. — (Modern world nations)
Includes bibliographical references and index.
  ISBN 0-7910-6778-5 (hardcover)
  1. Georgia (Republic)—Juvenile literature. I. Gritzner, Charles
F.
II. Title. III. Series.
  DK675.6 .P38 2002
  947.58—dc21

                         2002003712

Table of Contents

MODERN WORLD NATIONS

Republic of
Georgia

A seventeenth-century fortress and church on the military highway between Tbilisi and Ordzhonikidze.

CHAPTER 1

An Introduction to Georgia

A Georgian legend tells the story that when God divided Earth's surface among peoples, everyone except the Georgians received land. Deeply hurt by the apparent oversight, the Georgians invited God to come for a visit. When he arrived, the Georgians were not sullen and resentful. In fact, as is their custom, they were celebrating and full of joy. God joined them in their celebration and so enjoyed the visit, as the legend goes, that he decided to give the Georgians, or Kartvelians as they call themselves, something very special. God gave them the land between mountains and sea that he had reserved for himself—this land has been inhabited for millennia by the Georgian people and the beautiful country today bears their name.

For its size, Georgia is one of the world's most unique countries. Packed into its relatively small area—26,911 square miles (69,700 square kilometers), about the size of West Virginia or South Carolina—are an unsurpassed diversity of natural and cultural features. It is doubtful whether any other place on Earth can match Georgia's spectacular natural landscapes, its fascinating and complex history, or its rich and varied cultural heritage.

The origin of Georgia's name is not known. There is no evidence to suggest that it derives from Saint George, as some historians have suggested. Some sources indicate that the name comes from the Arabic and Persian words, Kurj and Gurj. Still others believe that it comes from an ancient Greek word translated to mean "farmers." Georgians, themselves, call their country Sakartvelo. Russians controlled Georgia for several centuries and in their language, the country is called Gruziia. But this controversy offers a splendid introduction to some of the problems in studying this fascinating land and people. Through time, many cultures have placed their imprint on Georgia. Nowhere, perhaps, is this more evident than in the country's place names. It is not at all uncommon for a Georgian place to be identified by four or five (and in some instances even more) different names, or variations of a single name. This confusing situation is the result of different cultures naming the same place, but each in its own language. In this book, place names that are most common in the West and in English usage will be used.

Georgia shares borders with Russia to the north, across the high Caucasus Mountains, Azerbaijan on the southeast, Armenia to the south, Turkey to the southwest, and the Black Sea coast to the west. Some historians place the country in the Middle East, even though as a dominantly Christian nation it seems to be misplaced within this Islam-dominated world. Others refer to it as the "Former Soviet Georgia," suggesting its close historical tie to its giant northern neighbor.

Perhaps nowhere is the confusion greater than in trying to determine whether Georgia is a European or Asiatic country. This question, too, suggests the great complexity of Georgia's

The Republic of Georgia shares borders with Russia to the north, across the high Caucasus Mountains, Azerbaijan on the southeast, Armenia to the south, Turkey to the southwest, and the Black Sea Coast to the west. It is frequently referred to as the "Former Soviet Georgia," which reflects the close historical ties Georgia has had with its giant neighbor to the north.

past; it also reveals a major flaw in the idea dividing the world into meaningful "continents." Clearly, there is no obvious natural or cultural break between Europe and Asia. The "line" dividing the two is historical and it has shifted many times; even today, not all scholars agree on its location. In the area affecting Georgia, most geographers use the crest of the Caucasus Mountains as the dividing line. This regional division, based on continents, places the country in Asia. Today, however, nearly all geographers, historians, and other social scientists use culture—a people's way of life—to divide the world into meaningful regions. Culturally and historically, Georgia has had much closer ties to Europe than it has to Asia. The majority of its people are European in terms of language, religion, political orientation, and many other traits. Their history, too, has been more closely tied to Europe than to Asia.

Another question is raised by Georgia's location relative to the Caucasus Mountains. Most Western literature refers to the region as "Transcaucasia," or the "Transcaucasus"—the area lying south of the Caucasus range and between the Black and Caspian Seas. These terms, however, are Western translations of the Russian word "Zakavkazje," meaning "The area beyond the Caucasus Mountain Range."

Georgians, as well as their neighboring Azerbaijanis and Armenians, strongly resent their regional identity being imposed by a Russian perspective carrying a biased political overtone. The name preferred by Georgians and others in the region is "South Caucasus" (with variations "South Caucasia," and "South Caucasian"). These preferred terms will be used in all contexts other than historical when referring to formerly Russian-held territory south of the Caucasus.

Historically, Georgia is both ancient and new. The earliest evidence of ancestral humans outside of African has been found in the country—dating back some 1.7 million years. Yet only having achieved its independence from the Soviet Union in 1991, Georgia is also one of the world's youngest countries.

Georgians consider themselves to be among the most "cultured" people on earth. Rather than an idle boast, there is considerable evidence to support this self-perception. Ancient Greeks, writing as early as the sixth century B.C., portrayed Georgia as a being a wealthy land with an advanced civilization. And Georgian advances in architecture, art, philosophy, music, and science predate the Italian Renaissance by over two centuries.

From its ancient past, to a troubled present, and a hopeful future, Georgia is one of the world's most fascinating lands. The diverse physical landscapes reach from Europe's highest peaks to the subtropical shores of the Black Sea. The following chapters will discuss the country's complex history and culture, its government and economy, its people and most interesting places, and its future.

Mount Kazbek, one of the towering peaks of the Caucasus Mountains. These mountains form an east-west boundary stretching nearly 700 miles between the Black and the Caspian seas.

CHAPTER

2

Physical
Landscapes

Georgia's physical landscapes offer great contrast and beauty. Few places of comparable size in the world can match the varied land features, climate, and ecosystems found within the country's 26,911 square mile area. Along Georgia's northern border with Russia, towering peaks of the Caucasus Mountains lie buried beneath a permanent blanket of snow and glacial ice. From these lofty heights, mountain slopes cascade southward into subtropical lowlands. In the west, the lush valley of the Rioni River slopes gradually toward the Black Sea; in central and eastern Georgia, the valley of the Mtkvari (Kura) River slopes eastward toward neighboring Azerbaijan.

Landforms and changes in elevation play a major role in creating Georgia's climate and ecosystems. From the crest of the

Caucasus Mountains to the shore of the Black Sea, elevation drops more than 16,000 feet (nearly 3 miles) in a
horizontal distance of about 60 miles. Within this short
span, sandwiched into micro-scale zones of increasing
elevation, one can find every climate and ecosystem that
occurs between subtropical coastal southern California
and or southern Florida, northward to the frigid Arctic—
a distance of some 6,000 miles.

Georgia's natural environment includes mountains,
valleys, coastal lands, caves, and other landform features.
Most important details of the country's weather and climate,
grasslands and forests, animal life, soils, and water features
will be explained. The natural environment has an important
effect on the people of this small country tucked away
between mountains and the sea in the land south of the
Caucasus—a remote corner of southwestern Asia.

The natural environment provides humankind with
its "life support system." Humans depend upon nature
and its resources—the water, air, soil, plant and animal life,
minerals, and the land for survival. Whereas natural elements
are essential to human life, environmental conditions do
not determine the way of life of a particular people. Culture—
what a people know and are able to do—is the primary factor
influencing how, or whether, people use the land and its
resources in a particular way.

In studying lands and peoples geographically, attention
is focused upon three important aspects of cultural ecology:
the first is how people of a particular culture (way of life)
adapt to the environment(s) they occupy; second, it is
important to understand how people "see" their environment, how they recognize, feel about, and use the land and
its resources; finally, attention must be given to the ways in
which the environment's appearance and usefulness have
been changed as human activity has etched its imprint on
the landscape.

Land Features

Mountains or other rugged features cover 80 percent of Georgia's land. To the north lie the Greater Caucasus Mountains. This towering range forms an east-west trending barrier stretching nearly 700 miles between the Black and Caspian Seas. Its crest forms the local boundary between the continents of Europe (to the north) and Asia (to the south). It also partially forms Georgia's border with its northern neighbor, Russia. Europe's highest peaks are found in the Caucasus, the most lofty being Russia's Mt. Elbrus. This towering giant rises to an elevation of 18,510 feet just a few miles north of Georgia's border. The highest peaks within Georgia are Mt. Shkhara (17,060 feet; 5,200 meters) and Mt. Kazbek (16,558 feet; 5,047 meters), both located near the Russian border.

The Great Caucasus Range is relatively young, geologically, and is of rather complex origin. First, Earth forces acting much like giant bulldozers pushed from both the north and south, creating two towering anticlines (upward folded ridges). Later, massive faulting and fiery volcanic activity added to the mountains' complexity. Upon this lofty rock base, thousands of glaciers, working over several million years, scoured the jagged, ruggedly beautiful, present-day mountain terrain. From these ice and glacier-clad peaks flow thousands of streams. Many have scoured deep and spectacular gorges. Dams have been built on a number of the streams to provide Georgia with hydroelectric power.

Some ancient mountain-building processes continue to work today, resulting in frequent and often severe earthquakes rocking the region. Snow avalanches and landslides also pose potentially deadly threats as they sweep down into occupied valley floors. In some places, roads pass through long sheds built to protect travelers from avalanches.

For centuries, the giant wall formed by the Caucasus has had both good and bad effects on this land and people. The mountains have severely limited north-south transportation and trade, as well as the migration of peoples and spread of ideas. Only three major roads cross the Caucasus within Georgia, and no railroad spans the range. To this day, the mountains separate quite different cultures, or ways of life. The mountains have also prevented bone-chilling Arctic air masses from reaching Georgia.

Southern Georgia's uplands are formed by the Lesser Caucasus Mountains. Between this low range and the Greater Caucasus is a trough that is the "heart" of Georgia. The lowland is divided into western and eastern sections by a low range of mountains. East-west travel across this central upland is gained through the long and difficult Suram Pass. This route, with its highest elevation at 2,700 feet, follows the twisting valley of the Mtkvari River (formerly called the Kura, the name by which it is still known in neighboring Azerbaijan).

Because of their importance to travel and trade, many mountain passes have cities located at each end. In Georgia, Kutaisi grew at the western end of the pass. This city is the gateway to the Colchis (Kolkhiz) Lowland. The Inguri and Rioni Rivers drain this broad, low-lying plain. At one time the region was a vast, malaria infested swamp largely covered with dense, jungle-like vegetation. Early in the 20th century, an ambitious development program was begun to make the land productive. It involved digging many miles of drainage canals and building levees (artificial banks) along the Rioni River and other streams in the region. The land is now protected from floods. Today, this once nearly useless region produces many valuable crops and supports a dense rural population. In the east, Georgia's capital and largest city, Tbilisi, is located at the other end of the pass. Here, the Mtkvari Valley begins to widen to form a broad, fertile plain between flanking mountains and plateaus.

In addition to its spectacular mountain scenery, Georgia is known for its many caves. Most caves form in limestone

The city of Kutaisi is at the western end of a mountain pass that was important to travel and trade in the region. It is located on the Rioni River.

rock, which is easily eaten away by the chemical action of water. Karst topography is the term by which geomorphologists (scientists who study land forms) recognize features resulting from this form of weathering and erosion. Georgia's limestone regions have been honeycombed into many caves and sink-holes. Nearly 300 caves have been discovered and explored. Some caverns rank among the world's largest and most spectacular. In some communities, water from underground cave-forming streams is tapped for home and village use. And for centuries, cool caves (some of which have ancient deposits of ice) have been use to store wine and other perishable items. Along the Black Sea coast, there are many sea caves. These caverns, scoured into steep rock cliffs by the constant pounding of waves, were once the hiding places of pirates who plundered Black Sea trading vessels.

Weather and Climate

Weather describes the atmosphere's condition at the moment; climate is the long-term average condition of weather. Georgia's climate is subtropical, with no monthly average temperature below 32 degrees F (0°C). Transcaucasia was the warmest part of the former Soviet Union. In fact, Georgia's warm Black Sea coast was one of the U.S.S.R.'s main tourist destinations. During winter months, the Caucasus Mountains protect the region from wintry blasts of cold air that sweep across Russia. In summer, the cooling waters of the Black Sea modify temperatures. Lowland Georgia lacks temperature extremes, either in summer or winter.

Perhaps the most important influence on both weather and climate in Georgia is the country's mountains. In general, temperatures drop about 3.5° F for every 1,000-foot increase in elevation (this explains why mountainous areas are much cooler than surrounding lowlands, and why high mountains remain snowcapped even during summer months). The city of Kutaisi, for example, may have a summer afternoon temperature of 80° F. Fifty miles north, in the mountains, temperatures may hover around freezing at higher elevations.

Precipitation (rain, snow, hail, or sleet) is greatest near the Black Sea, where several locations in the Colchis Lowland receive up to 110 inches of rain a year. Moisture decreases steadily the farther eastward one goes. The Mtkvari Valley east of Tbilisi receives only about 20 inches of precipitation each year. In mountain areas, moisture can vary greatly, depending on elevation and exposure to moisture-bearing winds. In highland areas, winter precipitation falls as snow.

Prevailing winds experience a monsoon-like seasonal change. During summer months, the wind blows from the Black Sea. It brings cool to moderate temperatures and a great deal of moisture. High humidity makes the air feel hot and sticky. In the winter, the pattern reverses as warm, dry, winds blow from the northeast. When blowing with great intensity, they are known as *foehn* winds (similar to the chinooks, or "snow eaters" in the interior of North America). Foehns sweep down mountain slopes, bringing unseasonable warm conditions to valleys below. Another wind, the *bora,* affects weather in the Colchis (Kolkhiz) Lowland. This cold, dry, winter wind can blow with the fury of a hurricane. It also can drop temperatures below freezing in a very short period of time, damaging or killing crops and bringing misery to people.

Much of lowland western Georgia enjoys a Mediterranean subtropical climate, much like that of coastal southern California. Both summers and winters are mild. Summer is the drier season, but enough rain falls even then to maintain a green landscape of plant life. Weather conditions make possible the growing of such warm weather crops as citrus fruits, tea, grapes (primarily for wine making), and cotton.

To the east, the climate becomes more continental, with higher and lower temperature extremes, and less precipitation. Most climatologists (scientists who study climate) classify the region as humid subtropical (similar to the southeastern United States, but somewhat drier).

Georgia does not experience severe storms. Heavy rain, dense fog, the bora and foehn winds, and winter blizzards at higher elevations can occasionally cause problems. Summer hailstorms can also cause damage to crops and property.

Vegetation, Animal Life, and Soils

Georgia has a remarkable variety of ecosystems. In the humid subtropical lowlands of the Colchis (Kolkhiz) Plain, plants thrive all year. Vegetation is dense and varied, with many evergreens, ferns, vines, and other fast-growing plants. Soils range in type from boggy, to red clay, and rich river-deposited alluvium. During recent decades, various drainage projects have turned this once marshy or swampy lowland into a fertile and productive agricultural area. Eastern Georgia is drier. Vegetation tends more toward scrub species, with fewer trees and more prairie (tall grass) and steppe (short grass). Soils tend toward gray and brown color and are fertile enough to support crop production and live-stock grazing.

About a third of Georgia is woodland. Trees found here and also in the United States include oak, alder, beech, and chestnut, as well as varieties of maple, ash, and fir. Eucalyptus trees have become common. This fast growing species was introduced from its native Australia and is widely used to line rural roadways. Woodland flowering plants include honey-suckle, azaleas, and rhododendrons. Natural vegetation, as is true of climate, changes rapidly with elevation. Lowland forests dominated by beech and chestnut gradually give way to needle leaf, coniferous, evergreen species at higher eleva-tions. Beginning at about 5,000 feet, birches mingle among conifers, and mountain "balds," or natural meadowlands, appear. This subalpine zone, used primarily for pasture, eventually gives way to the barren alpine conditions and eventual permanent fields of snow and ice.

Georgia has many animal species that are also common to the United States. Brown bears, wolves, and foxes roam the woodlands, as do porcupines and several types of wildcats. Squirrels and hares also are commonplace. Fishing in clear mountain lakes and rivers, you might catch a brown or rainbow trout, while watching an eagle soar overhead, or a wild turkey scratch for food on a hillside. Wild goats and antelope live in areas of higher elevation. In the subtropical lowlands, raccoons (introduced from the United States) and a large aquatic rodent, the nutria (introduced from Argentina), are common.

Water Features

Water availability is one of the most important geographic elements in determining land use and settlement patterns. Georgia is fortunate in having adequate and well-distributed water supplies.

Some 25,000 small streams begin in the Caucasus Mountains and flow generally southward into the lowlands. Here, most streams link with either of the country's two largest rivers—the Rioni, that drains into the Black Sea, or the Mtkvari (Kura), which flows into Azerbaijan and on to the Caspian Sea. Many streams are harnessed to produce electrical power. In regions of limestone rock, some streams disappear from the surface and flow underground. Their water eventually erodes away rock material to form caverns.

Georgia's dominant water feature is the Black Sea, which forms about 190 miles (310 km) of the country's western border. This body of water plays an important role in Georgia's climate. It is the primary source of moisture that falls as precipitation over land; its deep water also

The Black Sea is Georgia's most dominant water feature and, among other things, provides recreation to Georgians in the form of fishing and boating. The origin of the name "Black" has been attributed to many aspects of the sea, but no one really knows how it came by its name.

keeps temperatures moderate, neither too hot nor too cold, particularly in the western part of the country. Two of Georgia's five largest cities, Batumi and Sokhumi, are Black Sea ports. For centuries, the sea has been important for trade and fishing; in recent decades, it has become an important recreational destination as well.

The Black Sea has an interesting past. Through time, it has had different names. Each name tells us something about peoples' changing perceptions—what they believed and how they felt about this place. To ancient Greeks, the Black Sea was located at the edge of their known world. It was a remote place that was shrouded in mystery and explained in myth. They named it Pontus Axeinus, which means "inhospitable sea." Later, their known world expanded and the sea became more familiar to them. Its name became Pontus Euxinus, or "hospitable sea." According to Greek mythology, it was across these now friendly waters that Jason and the Argonauts sailed in search of the Golden Fleece—thought perhaps to have been in Colchis, Georgia's western lowland facing the Black Sea.

The origin of the name "Black" also is cloaked in mystery. According to some legends, it may have come from the skin color of a people (in myths, at least) who lived in the land of the Golden Fleece. Others suggest that the name may have originated with the sea's frequent storms. Winds can churn Black Sea water into a dark and treacherous surface; to sailors, it appeared as being "black" and inhospitable. A third theory has the name coming from the water of the sea, itself. The Black Sea is unique among the world's water bodies. There are two layers of water, each having a different density. A heavily saline bottom layer is stagnant. It has little movement, contains heavy concentrations of hydrogen sulfide, and has no marine life. The top layer is much less saline and therefore is "lighter" than the water below. It supports marine life, including many kinds of fish. Finally, some scientists have suggested that the hydrogen sulfides make the water appear darker, hence,

The defining features of the Republic of Georgia are the Caucasus Mountains that lie along the northern border with Russia, the lush valley of the Rioni River that slopes gradually to the Black Sea, and the valley of the Mtkvari River that slopes eastward toward neighboring Azerbaijan. Mountains or other rugged terrain cover over 80 percent of Georgia's land.

"black." It is doubtful that we will ever know how the sea got its name.

Environmental Concerns

Before 1991, Georgia was a republic within the Soviet Union. Little attention was given to the region's growing environmental pollution. In 1994, a new government office was formed—the Ministry of Protection of the Environment. It included a central environmental information and research agency. Since it was created, much more attention has been given to environmental concerns.

Overgrazing, erosion, and waste disposal have posed problems for centuries. During recent decades, Black Sea pollution has become a major environmental and health concern. Nearly 75 percent of Georgia's coastal water is heavily contaminated with health-endangering bacteria. Only about 20 percent of the raw sewage from coastal cities is treated before being released into the sea. The tourist industry, in particular, has been hard hit by this coastal pollution. Another environmental problem confronting Georgians is the civil conflict involving South Ossetia and Abkhazia, autonomous regions within the Georgian Republic. These military actions also have taken their toll on local environmental conditions.

A Pleasant and Varied Landscape

When tallying the plusses and minuses of Georgia's natural landscape, the country comes out far ahead. Other than the higher elevations of the Caucasus, all of its land is inhabited and is in some way productive. It lacks extremes of temperature and precipitation. Georgia has ample water supplies, fairly good soils throughout most of its area, and rich deposits of several mineral resources. Other than the polluted waters of the Black Sea coast, its environmental problems are not as challenging as those found in most other former Soviet Socialist Republics.

The statue of the fifth-century Georgian king, Vakhtang Gorgaslan, overlooks the capital of Tbilisi, which was established by him.

3

Georgia Through Time

Georgia holds the distinction of being one of the world's oldest, yet one of its youngest, places. An ancient river bluff archaeological site near Dmanisi has yielded bones of human-like skulls dating back some 1.7 million years. They are the oldest human fossils of ancestral humans ever found outside of Africa. On the other hand, it was not until 1991 that Georgia broke free from the former Soviet Union to become an independent country.

Because of its crossroads location amidst many great empires, Georgia has a complex history. The country and its culture are the products of kaleidoscopic changes, occurring over millennia, and often imposed by external agents and their influence. Through time, numerous migrations of people have passed through the region. So, too, have the military forces of many distant empires.

Both have left their indelible imprint on Georgia's landscape and culture. This is evident in the country's diverse ethnic, linguistic, religious, agricultural, and architectural traits. The most recent external influence was the seven-decade stretch during which Georgia labored under Soviet political and economic control. During this period, however, the country's culture and society remained relatively unchanged. Georgia's distance from Moscow, and the isolation provided by the Caucasus Mountains, limited Russia's cultural influence in the region.

Ancient History

Little is known of the earliest humans who occupied the land of present-day Georgia. Archaeological evidence suggests that several hundred thousand years ago, humans inhabited both the Black Sea coastal region and interior lowlands and highlands. They were few in number and left scant evidence of their presence. Almost certainly, they lived by hunting and gathering foods and raw materials for their diet, shelter, and clothing. They were skilled in the use of stone to make tools and weapons. In all probability, these early people were migratory and had few material possessions. By constantly moving, they did not over-harvest local natural resources.

About 7,000 years ago, a Neolithic (New Stone Age) culture appeared in the area of present-day Georgia. They soon began working with metals—first copper and later bronze (a metal alloy composed of copper and tin)—and were renown for the excellence of their pottery. By the second millennium B.C., the union of two strong tribes—the Colchis in the west and Diakhi in the east—brought wealth and power to the region. Bronze tools and weapons, fine pottery, and ornate artworks made of gold have been found in excavated tombs believed to be those of tribal leaders from this era. Through the millennia, these various people mixed with many others who migrated into, or through, the region. From this diverse stock evolved today's Georgian people.

Archaeology and history both focus upon the past. Archaeologists study history using ancient human remains and artifacts; historians emphasize documents—primarily the printed record—in their study. The first documented (historical) record of Georgia appears in the 11th or 12th century B.C. It is in an Assyrian reference to a captured local king named Sieni. The earliest documented Georgian tribes were people inhabiting the area soon after the collapse of the Hittite Empire, around 1190 B.C. During this period, a tribe known as the Mushki migrated from eastern Anatolia (in present day Turkey) into what is now western Georgia.

Early Georgian Kingdoms

The territory of Georgia has changed frequently through time. At times, it has been integrated into vast empires controlled by distant civilizations. At other times, it has been fragmented into small territories controlled by different foreign forces, or local ethnic groups. Georgians call themselves Kartveli and their country Sakartvelo, meaning "place of the Georgians." The latter word, however, was not used until the 11th century. It was not until then that the region's people were united, and even this joining proved to be temporary. Throughout much of Georgia's history the Surami Mountains have been a barrier dividing the country into eastern and western kingdoms, each with its own culture and unique history.

Kolkhida Kingdom. The earliest Georgian kingdom, Kolkhida (Colchis), emerged in the Colchis Lowland bordering the Black Sea during the late Bronze Age (15th to 8th century B.C.). The setting was ideal. The Black Sea allowed access to the "outer world." The lowland, itself, was fertile, sheltered, subtropical, and adequately moist. Through it ran the River Phasis of antiquity (today's Rioni River). The

Kolkhida were very successful farmers, raising a variety of grains, fruits and vegetables, and livestock. Their linen was so fine that the Ancient Greek geographer and historian, Herodotus, referred to it in his writings. They also were skilled metal smiths, smelting and casting iron, copper, and bronze, and as early as the ninth century B.C.—long before these skills were mastered in Europe.

So advanced were the Kolkhidians that word of their lofty achievements spread to distant lands. Ancient Greek legends told of a distant and fabulously wealthy land. Supposedly, it was to Kolkhida that Jason and the Argonauts traveled and there they stole the Golden Fleece from King Aietes with the help of his daughter, Medea. Historians believe that the "Land of the Golden Fleece" actually existed, but they still argue over the actual location of this renowned place. Interestingly enough, people living in the Caucasus during this era supposedly used sheepskins to trap gold particles found in the sands of mountain streambeds. Sand would lodge in the wool, but the heavier gold would settle deep within the fleece. When the skins were removed from the stream, dried out, and beaten, the precious metal was released. This story serves as a reminder that at least some "myths" are, in actuality, the vague recollections of things and events that actually happened in the distant past.

From about 600 B.C., Greek civilization was gaining power and expanding its sphere of influence. Greeks colonies began to appear in what is now coastal Georgia. Their trade and administrative centers included the present-day coastal cities of Sukhumi, Batumi, and Ochamchira. Ancient Greeks developed an unparalleled level of civilization and culture during the half-millennium prior to dawn of the Christian era. Georgians benefited in many ways from the long-term diffusion (flow) of Greek ideas, skills, and material traits, which they were able to integrate into their own culture.

Greek colonies began to appear in what is now coastal Georgia from about 600 B.C. on. These amphoras, used to carry goods such as olive oil and wine, were made in 430-408 B.C. They were discovered in the Black Sea where an ancient Greek city was once located and reflect the influence of Greek civilization in this area.

Iberian (Kartli) Empire. After the Kingdom of Kolkhida was destroyed during the fourth to third centuries B.C., another Georgian kingdom, Iberia (in Georgian, Kartli), was established. The Iberian Empire (not to be confused with the southwest European peninsula of the same name) took root in Georgia east of the Surami Mountains. Its base was Mtskheta, a city located at the southern end of the Caucasus' Daryal Pass and at the eastern gateway of the Surami Pass. This ideal geographical position placed Mtskheta on the crossroad of trade between Eastern Europe, the Middle East, central Asia, and both the Black and Caspian Seas. Kartli-Iberia soon became the core of the evolving Georgian nation. It was able to integrate many area tribes into a kingdom of which many present-day Georgians are direct decedents.

Romans and Christians
(First Century B.C.—Fourth Century A.D.)

In the first century B.C., Roman forces invaded the territory of Georgia. After a brief war in 65 B.C., peace was established between (Georgian) Iberia and Rome. Georgia became a part of the expanding Roman Empire, a status it held for the next several centuries. Georgians largely accepted Roman control and influence. So much so, in fact, the Romans gave Georgians many rights as their allies. Ultimately, because of this arrangement, Iberia's power and influence increased. Its economy prospered because of the continuing importance of its location on a major trade route between India and other locations to the east, and Rome to the west.

By the third century A.D., however, Georgian kingdoms had again weakened. In the west, Kolkhida had been under Roman control for a century. In the east, Iberia had fallen under the domination of aggressive expansion by a new Persian (Iranian) ruling dynasty. Christianity had taken root among some Georgian peoples during the period of Roman domination. Now, non-Christian Persians sought to take control of all lands located south of the Caucasus and between the Black and Caspian Seas. This presented a major threat to the existence of Georgia's kingdoms and culture. Endangered, Georgians turned to Rome for help.

The first step was to declare Christianity as the official

When Christianity was first introduced into Georgia in the first century, it was not a major influence. But later Georgia became one of the first countries in the world to make Christianity its state religion. This tomb of King Marian at the 11th century Church of Samtravo, at Mtskheta, is adorned with frescoes of the saints that are among the greatest achievements of Georgian religious painters.

religion in Kolkhida and Iberia. Although Christianity had been introduced into Georgia during the first century, it was not of major importance in the region. In the 330s, King Marian III of Eastern Georgia adopted Christianity as the official religion of Iberia, and Colchis soon followed. Georgia thus became one of the first countries in the world to elevate Christianity to the status of the state (official) religion.

Unfortunately, the church destroyed much of the existing Georgian literature, and with it much of the country's documented heritage.

By the beginning of the fifth century, Romans no longer were in a position to help the Georgians. Their empire was being invaded. Germanic tribes had successfully disrupted Roman trade routes throughout much of Europe and even invaded Italy as far south as Rome. Luckily for the Georgians, a new king, Vakhtang Gorgaslan, rose to become a powerful leader in the fight against Persians. He also was successful in unifying the Georgian people and in expanding Georgian territory by conquest. During his reign, King Vakhtang established Tbilisi, which ultimately became Georgia's capital and largest city. Soon after the king's death in battle, Persians swept in and gained control over most of Georgia's eastern territories. They were helped in this conquest by disunity among the region's many kingdoms and feudal lords. Western Georgia had for some time been under control of the Eastern Roman Empire (or Byzantium). But during the sixth century the region was in political turmoil, as it changed hands between Byzantines and Persians many times.

Middle Ages (5th–11th Centuries)

Few countries in the world have a more complex and difficult history than does Georgia. The land has seldom been at peace. During the more than 600-year duration of the so-called (European) Middle Ages, Georgia continued to experience almost continuous turbulence.

Arab Dominance. After several centuries of conflict between Romans and Persians over control of Georgia, a new external force began to threaten this troubled land. Beginning in the early 630s, Muslim Arabs left their home-land on the Arabian Peninsula. They swept through much of the Middle East, conquering established kingdoms throughout the region. By 655, much of central Georgia (called Kartli) had fallen to Arab control. Their emir (leader) established residence in Tbilisi, thereby further establishing this city's dominance as a regional political and trading center. Over the next several centuries, however, the Arab grip on Georgia gradually weakened. This provided an opportunity for local feudal rulers to form a number of small, independent kingdoms.

Emergence of a Unified Georgia. During the 11th century, Byzantine forces briefly gained control over Georgia, as did the Selchukid Turks. This time, foreign rule was short-lived. Toward the end of the 11th century, Christian Crusaders from Western Europe began to exert their influence on the Holy Land and Middle East. A new Georgian ruler decided to cut Turkish rule and to unite the country. In 1122, King David IV was successful in grasping Tbilisi from the Arabic emirs and the rest of Georgia from the Byzantines and Turks. He became the first king to control all Georgian territory; his empire expanded to include Armenia in the south, and Azerbaijan eastward to the shores of the Caspian Sea. For his military success in (re)building the Georgian kingdom and expanding its territory, King David IV got his nickname "The Builder."

Georgia's "Golden Era" (12th–13th Centuries)

The 12th and early 13th centuries are recognized as having been Georgia's "Golden Era." The early 1100s brought liberation from foreigners, political unification, and cultural reconstruction. It was a period of political and economic stability, and unprecedented cultural growth. Numerous advances in education, economy, art, literature, architecture, music, and other aspects of cultural attainment characterized the "golden era." Georgia's political influence also had spread widely. It spanned lands on both sides of the Caucasus; it reached southward into northwestern Persia (Iran) and northeastern Turkey; and it bridged the entire area south of the Caucasus and between the Black and Caspian Seas. The Georgian kingdom reached its height of power during the rule of Queen Tamar (1184-1213). Not long after her reign and a century of stability and prosperity, Georgia once again fell under the foreign rule and into cultural stagnation.

During the early 1200s, horse-mounted Mongolian warriors from central Asia began an enormous expansion. Their invasion of Georgia in 1236 marked the beginning of another long era of strife, fragmentation, and decline in the region. Georgia became part of a huge Mongol Empire that ultimately reached from central Europe eastward to the Pacific Ocean, and southward into northwestern India. It became the largest conterminous (having the same boundary) empire in human history. Mongolian rule of Georgia continued into the 14th century. King Giorgi V (1314-1346) finally liberated Georgia from Mongolian rulers, and Georgia once again began the difficult task of rebuilding. But even this brief period of restoration was soon interrupted.

During the last decades of the 14th century, another vast empire of conquest was taking shape to the south of Georgia. A Muslim warrior, Timur (Tamerlane), conquered lands stretching from the eastern Mediterranean, eastward to northern India, and northward to the Caucasus. In 1386, he entered Georgia and destroyed Tbilisi, thus ending the last attempt to restore Georgia's "golden era" of feudal society.

Meanwhile, other Christian kingdoms within southwest Asia, including those established by the Crusades, had been destroyed or, like Byzantium, had been seriously weakened. Linkages between Georgians and Eastern European Christians were severed. The next several centuries were marked by complete disintegration of Georgia as a united country. And once again, it came under the pressure of empires seeking to expand into its territory.

The Ottoman Empire, centered on Turkey's Anatolia Plateau, was beginning to spread during the mid-15th century. Ottoman Turks had destroyed Byzantium and captured Constantinople and they now began to spread in all directions. In Persia, a powerful dynasty began to set its sights on westward and northward expansion toward Transcaucasia. During the 15th and 16th centuries, Georgia again found itself in the middle of a fierce battle for domination by foreign powers. The destruction inflicted by constant military conflicts degraded both the Georgian landscape and way of life. The region's economy was in shambles, education was at a standstill, artistic expression all but disappeared, and society was in turmoil. In the mid-16th century, the Persian and Ottoman empires decided to divide Georgia. By mutual agreement, western Georgia went to the Turks and the eastern part of the country went to the Persians. Historically, this proved to be the final partitioning of Georgia. After the division, resistance by the proud Georgians never ceased. They constantly gave both Persians and Turks a great deal of trouble.

In 1556 another force appeared on the borders of the region. After Czarist Russian troops captured Astrakhan, a city just north of Caucasus, they became a third possible player in the geopolitical tug-of-war over Georgia. Russian forces made some contact with Georgian kings who were fighting for independence from the Persians and Ottoman Turks. Nothing came of the Russian presence and fighting between Georgians and their oppressors continued to rage for several centuries. According to some estimates, as many as 200,000 Georgians died as a result of military conflict during this period. Not until the early 1700s, under the leadership of King Vakhtang VI, did Georgia return to a peaceful state in which cultural, economic, and political progress could be achieved. Unfortunately, this stability was short-lived. The struggle against the Turks and Persians continued. Dagistanis were tribesmen who also joined in the conflict with a series of devastating raids. By the end of the 1700s, Georgia was under a constant state of siege from without and within. The country was impossible to rule. Various feudal and political groups engaged in seesaw-like struggles for power.

Russian Georgia (1800-1917)

By the late 1700s, Georgians decided that the only way they could protect their land from constant attack was to seek help from the Russians. A treaty was signed in 1783 that supposedly committed Russia to protecting Georgia from outside forces. Georgians expected the Russians, who also were Christians, to help protect them from Muslim-dominated hostile powers. Unfortunately, when Persians invaded Georgia in 1795, Russia did not come to their defense. Instead, Russian Czar Alexander I decided to annex Georgia, and his troops successfully invaded the country in 1799. Soon thereafter, in 1801, Russia claimed Georgia as part of its own territory. This event marked the end of Georgia's various kingdoms and began two centuries during which Georgia's destiny was tied to Russia.

During the 19th century, Russia was successful in annexing Georgian territory that had been under Ottoman rule. After wars with Turks and Persians, Russia was able to spread its rule over the territory bordering the Caucasus Mountains and between the Black and Caspian Seas. But, constant rebellions involving numerous ethnic groups, including Georgians, required a strong Russian military presence in the region. The greatest resistance to Russian control came from the Muslim tribes that did not want to accept Christian rule. Many rebels fought against Russians. The best known of all was Shamil, a Muslim warlord from neighboring Dagistan, who successfully led anti-Russian resistance in the north Caucasus for several decades. Nothing, however, could stop the integration of Caucasus nations into the Russian Empire.

By the end of 19th century, rebellious forces had been eliminated from the region.

As occurred throughout Europe toward the end of 19th century, nationalistic feelings also began to rise in Georgia. Numerous movements and organizations, including Marxists, began to surface on the political scene. In Russia and Georgia, it was particularly the Marxist movement that gained in popularity. Support for revolutionary movements spread rapidly. People were tired of the autocratic czarist Russian regime. During these turbulent years, one Georgian, in particular, stands out for his involvement in the Bolshevik (Communist) party. His name was Iosif Jugashvili, better known as Joseph Stalin.

Soviet Period (1920s-1991)

World War I (1914-1918) temporarily stopped revolutionary activities and increased military efforts. Georgia became the battleground for Russian and Turkish fighting for political control of the South Caucasus region. Russia's government and its history changed abruptly, however, in 1917 when the Bolshevik (Communist) Revolution overthrew the centuries old, oppressive czarist regime. Georgians, meanwhile, used the opportunity of a weakened Russia to their advantage. In May 1918, the National Council of Georgia declared the country's independence. After 117 years, Georgia's statehood was restored. Unfortunately, the new Georgian independent republic survived only three years. In February 1921, the Soviet Army invaded Georgia, captured Tbilisi, forced its leaders to leave the country, and took control of the government.

The next political move came in 1922, when Georgia was integrated into the Transcaucasian Soviet Federated Socialist Republic (S.F.S.R.)—a step that made Georgia, and neighboring lands of Armenia and Azerbaijan, a part of the Soviet Union. In 1936, the Transcaucasian S.F.S.R. was terminated

When Russia's Czarist regime was abruptly replaced by the Communist Revolution in 1917, Georgia's National Council seized the moment to declare their own independence. But by 1921 Georgians again found themselves under the rule of the Russian state.

and Georgia became an autonomous Soviet Republic. Under Soviet domination, the republic's economy improved some-what, as did the education of its young. But Georgia was not immune to political repression during Stalinism. Even though both Stalin and his chief of secret police, Lavrenti

Pavlovich Beria, were Georgians, many of their fellow countrymen were sent to the Gulag (Siberian prisons).

Germans invaded the Soviet Union in 1941 and many Georgians joined the Soviet army to defend the U.S.S.R. against Nazis forces. Approximately 10 percent of the republic's population—an estimated 300,000 to 400,000 people—died during World War II. But Georgia was saved from German occupation.

After the end of World War II and Stalin's death in 1953, Georgian nationalism once again began to rise. As had happened so often before, and at the hand of so many different foreign powers, the quest for freedom from Soviet control was immediately suppressed. The desire for independence nonetheless continued to burn deeply in the hearts and minds of Georgia's people. Until the fall of the Soviet Union in 1991, Georgians continued to be criticized by the Soviets as being troublesome renegades. During the 1970s, another Georgian personality appeared on the Soviet political scene. His name was Edward (Eduard) Shevardnadze, and he was a skilled and widely respected politician who soon became the Soviet Union's minister of foreign relations and a world famous diplomat. Eventually, he was to play a very important role in Georgia, as well.

Independence

During the latter half of the 1980s, Soviet leader Mikhail Gorbachev introduced many reforms that created an atmosphere of greater openness and freedom in the Soviet Union. Georgians quickly realized that Gorbachev's policies might have opened a door of opportunity for seeking national independence. In the fall of 1990, a multiparty election was held in Georgia, an event that ended decades of single party government. Zviad Gamsakhurdia, a former Soviet dissident, assumed leadership and in 1991 organized a referendum for independence from the Soviet Union. The vote resulted in

Georgia declaring its independence from the U.S.S.R. Although independence was declared on April 9, 1991, it did not become a reality until the Soviet Union was disbanded on December 26 of that year. Unfortunately, the political situation within the newly independent Republic of Georgia quickly deteriorated. Politicians and other forces in opposition to Gamsakhurdia asked for new elections. Many opposition leaders were arrested, resulting in open rebellion and the start of armed civil conflict. Gamsakhurdia finally was forced out of office and out of the country.

Meanwhile, native-son Edward Shevardnadze returned to Georgia and became the country's temporary leader. His influence hastened the process of gaining international recognition of Georgia as an independent state. By July 1992, Georgia was accepted as a member of the United Nations. During the first part of the 1990s, Georgia experienced major problems between its government and several of the country's ethnic groups. Separatist movements in the South Ossetia and Abkhazia autonomous regions threatened secession from Georgia. Conflicts escalated creating thousands of casualties and many more refugees. In 1992, with the help of Russian president Boris Yeltsin, a ceasefire was declared in South Ossetia. However, in the far northwestern tip of Georgia, home of the separatist Abkhazian Autonomous Republic, clashes continued. With help from the United Nations and Russia, a shaky ceasefire was finally declared in this conflict as well.

After presidential elections in 1995 and 2000, in which Edward Shevardnadze achieved victory, the situation in Georgia has become somewhat more stabilized. But tensions still exist. In late 2001, sporadic fighting once again broke out between government forces and the secession-minded Abkhazians. As the year drew to a close, President Shevardnadze fired his entire cabinet, plunging the country into yet another political crisis.

At his swearing-in ceremony in Tbilisi on November 26, 1995 Edward Shevardnadze stands on a podium behind a group of men dressed in Georgian national costumes. He was elected president of Georgia by a wide margin in the election.

The Georgian State Dance Company is world famous for its performances of traditional dances.

CHAPTER

4

Land of Cultural Contrast

G eorgia's people are as diverse as the land they occupy. The country is home to many different groups of people, each with its own heritage and strong sense of self-identity. Georgia takes its name from the ethnic group that represents more than half of the country's population: Georgians. But many other people share this land with them. Cultural diversity has strengthened Georgia in many ways. Unfortunately, it has also resulted in conflict.

Georgia has been both blessed and cursed by its geographical location. It is situated on major east-west and (through passes in the Caucasus) north-south routes linking Europe and Asia. Historically, many early migrating peoples settled within the region, often seeking refuge in valleys hidden away in the flanks of the Caucasus. Through time, many powerful empires have bordered Georgia. People of Transcaucasia have benefited from the flow of ideas from other cultures. But many of these empires had a goal of territorial expansion—including the area occupied by Georgia. From Mediterranean Europe came Greeks and later Romans; from the south, at different times over many centuries, came Parthians, Byzantines, Persians, Arabs, and Ottoman Turks; and from the north, troops from central Asia, including those led by Genghis Khan and Tamerlane, swept southward into the region. Most recently, in the 1800s, Russians invaded Georgia. Each group left its own imprint on what became the cultural mosaic of today's Georgian people.

Since the breakup of the Soviet Union in 1991, Georgia has experienced ethnic conflicts in Abkhazia and South Ossetia. These civil skirmishes have left a heavy mark on the country's landscape, population, and political stability. In many ways, Georgia's situation is similar to that of the Balkan States after their independence. The iron rule of the Communist Party, backed by the powerful Soviet military, prevented hostilities between different ethnic groups. Once free of Communist rule, however, long-simmering antagonisms between ethnic groups began to boil over into open conflict. Nonetheless, when all factors are weighed, Georgia is much richer from its cultural diversity. In this chapter, you will learn about Georgia's people and their culture.

Language and Ethnicity

A single place or feature shown on a map or discussed in a book may be identified by as many as four or five different names, and a single name may have several different spellings. Additionally, local names are often converted into a simplified version when printed in English. This problem stems from the country's history and ethnic diversity. Not only does each ethnic group have its own language, but in Georgia several different alphabets are used as well.

Language is perhaps the most reliable indicator of culture and ethnicity. Nearly all of the ethnic groups discussed below take their name from their language. Before spotlighting the differences that exist in the way of life of Georgia's people, some important terms must be defined. Culture is a people's "way of life" and includes everything that a culturally bound group has, thinks, and does. Examples of culture include language, religion, architecture, diet, dress, and how they make their living. Nationality is a group or person's self-identity. It is the answer to the question, "What are you?" Ethnicity is a more difficult term to define. Most geographers use the concept when referring to a minority population living among a larger culture. In culturally divided Georgia, for example, each culturally different society is an ethnic group.

A final concept is understanding many of the world's, and Georgia's, present-day problems—is the distinction between the ideas of nation, state, and nation-state. A nation is the territory occupied by a nationality of people. A state, on the other hand, is defined as being a politically governed territory (such as Georgia). A nation-state, then, is the territory occupied by a nationality of peoples that also is self-governing. In Georgia, conflict results from there being many nationalities (ethnic groups) existing within a single state. As minority populations, they have little say in how they are governed. They feel powerless and therefore are resentful.

Georgia's ethnic pattern resembles a patchwork quilt. An estimated 70 percent of the country's population is ethnic Georgian, the people and culture from which the country takes its name. Georgian is an ancient language. Its unique alphabet, created in the third century A.D., is one of 14 existing alphabets in the world. The language belongs to Kartvelian, a little-known linguistic group that is surrounded by mystery in terms of its origin or spread. Some scholars, for example, believe that Georgian is related to the language spoken by the Basques in northern Spain. And many linguists believe that some of the northern Caucasic languages also share the same roots.

Several other ethnic groups have significant representation, amounting to another 25 percent of the total population.

The Georgian language has a unique alphabet that was developed in the 3rd century A.D. This inscribed stone at Oubissk Monastery near Kutaisi is an example of the appearance of the writing.

Additionally, about 5 percent of Georgia's population is composed of much smaller ethic groups. These small minority populations are scattered about the country, often living in remote areas. Because of their isolation, some of them have been successful in preserving their culture and identity for centuries.

Armenians are the second largest ethnic group in Georgia. They number about 8 percent of the population. Culturally, Armenians are quite similar to ethnic Georgians with whom they have shared the same religion and living space for centuries. Many Armenians live in southeastern Georgia, close to the country's border with neighboring Armenia.

Russians account for about 6 percent of the population and are Georgia's third largest ethnic group. The history of Russians in Georgia is somewhat different than that of other peoples, because their immigration (moving to a country) was much more recent. Prior to the dawn of the 19th century, very few Russians lived in Georgia. But in the early 1800s Georgia was integrated into the Russian empire and the Russian migration began. During seven decades of Soviet dominance, the number of Russians living and working in Georgia increased substantially. But during the past decade, since Georgia achieved its independence from the Soviet state, many Russians have left the country to return to their homeland. Most remaining Russians are those who became culturally and socially integrated into Georgian society. They live in cities where industrial, political, economic, and educational institutions are located.

Azeris, concentrated in eastern Georgia along the border with Azerbaijan, account for another 5 to 6 percent of the population. Unlike the Armenians who share much in common with ethnic Georgians, Azeris are different in many ways. Neighboring Azerbaijan, also one of the former Soviet Republics that is now an independent country, is homeland to most Azeris. As is often the case, however, political borders (state) do not often follow ethnic borders (nation). Azeris are both ethnically and religiously different than Georgians and Armenians. They belong to the Turkish people that migrated from Central Asia hundreds of years ago and inhabited areas between the Black Sea and Caspian Sea. Azeris and Turks are closely related cousins, a fact that is evident in their language and other aspects of culture. Their religion, for example, is Islam, the same as in other Turkish-influenced countries.

Numbering about 3 percent of the population, Ossetians are another small, but important, ethnic group. These hardy people are descendents of warriors from Central Asia who settled in the foothills of the Caucasus Mountains nearly three thousand years ago. As a people, Ossetians are divided by the Greater Caucasus: North Ossetians live in Russia on the northern flanks of the Caucasus; South Ossetians live in Georgia. Since 1990, however, the South Ossetians have claimed their independence from Georgia. This has resulted in

This 86-year-old veteran of World War II is showing off his dance style. He is a member of the Abkhazian ethnic group, which has been seeking independence from Georgia. They comprise approximately 1.78% of the Georgian population.

a long and bitter conflict between the Georgian government and the fewer than 100,000 Ossetians who seek to be free of Georgian political dominance.

Abkhazians are the final ethnic group, making up more than 1 percent of Georgia's population. Most of them live in Georgia's autonomous republic of Abkhazia in the remote northwestern part of the country. They, too, seek independence from Georgia and the result, as with the South Ossetians, has been a violent civil conflict.

A number of other very small ethnic groups and tribes also live in Georgia. Their numbers vary, but they stand apart because they have managed to preserve their cultural distinctiveness, including their language. Such groups include Karts, Megrels, Chans, and Swans, all Georgian tribal peoples, and nonnative Georgians, including Greeks, Jews, and Kurds.

POPULATION BY NATIONALITY		
NATIONALITY	QUANTITY	%
Georgian	3,787,400	70.13%
Russian	341,200	6.32%
Ossetian	164,100	3.04%
Abkhazian	95,900	1.78%
Kurt	33,300	0.62%
Armenian	437,200	8.10%
Jew	24,800	0.46%
Azerbaijani	307,600	5.70%
Ukrainian	52,400	0.97%
Greek	100,300	1.86%
Others	56,500	1.05%
Total	**5,400,700**	**100.00%**

Source: Parliament of Georgia (est. 2000)

Religion

Christianity and Islam are the major religions of Georgia. Over 85 percent of the population is Christian, and about 10 percent is Muslim (followers of Islam). Such numbers, however, are relatively meaningless. During the seven decades of Soviet control, religion was strongly suppressed. Today, few of the country's people regularly practice their religion. Most Georgians are of the Georgian Orthodox faith, whereas most Russians remaining in the country are Russian Orthodox. The majority of Azeris, and some Abkhazians, are Muslims. Judaism

The Church of the Virgin stands on the grounds of the 12th century Monastery of Gelati, at Kutaisi. By the 4th century A.D., King Marian III believed he had witnessed two miracles and thereupon accepted Christianity as his faith.

is practiced by a small number of Georgians, most of whom live in large cities such as Tbilisi and Kutaisi.

Until early in the fourth century A.D., people living in what is today Georgia believed in and practiced various ethnic faiths (belief systems practiced by individual ethnic groups). In 330 A.D., however, two strange events helped make Georgians among the earliest people to accept Christianity. According to tradition, Christianity came to Georgia in 330 A.D., when a devout slave woman, who became known as

Saint Nino, supposedly cured the Queen of Iberia of some unknown illness. Soon thereafter, Georgian King Marian III is said to have witnessed a "second miracle" while on a hunting trip. The two events led the king to accept Christianity, which soon became the religion of most Georgian people. As was true throughout the Christian realm, the church played an important role in developing a written language. Writing was essential for the keeping of church records and preparation of religious texts.

Islam came to Georgia several centuries later, first as a result of Arabic expansion into the region, and later from Persia and Turkey. Today both Shiite and Sunnite Muslims live and practice their religion in Georgia. The arrival of Islam placed Georgia in the difficult position of being on the border between the world's two great faiths—Christianity to the west and Islam to the south and east. Nonetheless, Georgia has a tradition of religious tolerance.

Other Aspects of Georgian Culture

Over their long history, Georgians developed a rich and quite distinct culture. Language and religion are but two important aspects of their way of life; there are many more. Two other important elements of culture are how people make a living and how they are governed. Other aspects of the Georgian culture are discussed in chapter 7, which gives a glimpse of the country's regions and contemporary life. Here, attention is focused on architecture, the arts, and foodways.

Architecture. Georgia's architecture, like so many other aspects of its culture, has evolved over centuries and from many outside influences. Students of architecture marvel at the adaptability of the region's structures. Materials, design, and construction are all extremely well adapted to the environment and the needs of inhabitants. Early cultures that helped mold Georgia's architectural landscape include the Greeks, Romans, Arabs, and Turks. Stone and wood are the primary materials used in building. Earth and animal skins are other resources that have been used by traditional groups. The most traditional Georgian structure is the *darbazi*. This ancient dwelling was described in the first century B.C. as being typical of those found in the Colchian Lowland. Traditionally, the building was made of horizontally laid logs, with walls tapering toward a cupola form roof. Its major features include an open hearth in its center and the unique roof that serves both as a skylight and an outlet for smoke.

In mountainous regions, traditional peasant houses included a high, stone-built, tower. From the tower, residents could see approaching enemies and also be in a better position to use weapons in their defense.

Perhaps the most unique architectural innovation to develop in Georgia is its church-building style. As early as the sixth century A.D., churches were built with cupolas. Architectural historians believe that this type of construction had its origin in Georgian domestic architecture dating back to the third millennium B.C. Forms of ancient structures that inspired church builders survive today in the darbazi structures. Secular architecture during the Middle Ages included many towers and fortresses built on mountain steps. As is true of many other aspects of Georgian culture, architecture reached its golden age during the 12th and 13th centuries. Since then, many outside influences have been integrated into Georgian architecture. In the 19th century, Russian influence began to appear in buildings. Influence from the north increased greatly after the Soviet takeover. This included so-called Stalinist style architecture that began to have an impact on Tbilisi and other cities during the mid-20th century.

Georgia has impressive historical and contemporary architecture. Ancient castles, ornate churches, homes of various styles and materials, rustic bridges, and many other structures attest to the creativity, art, and skill of the Georgian people, now as in the past.

The Arts. Georgian art, like its architecture and literature, also reached its high point during the 12th and 13th centuries. The Orthodox religion played an important role in artistic achievement during this period. Frescoes of saints, influenced perhaps by Byzantines, represent the greatest achievements of Georgian religious painters. Nonreligious painting, most influenced by Persians, also reached its peak during this era. The ravages of time and changing political circumstances have taken their toll on Georgian art. Nineteenth-century Russians, in particular, destroyed much of Georgia's religious art. Some examples of beautiful artwork, often little more than fragments, still can be seen in churches in perhaps a dozen Georgian communities.

Literature. Prior to the 10th century, most literature was religious in nature. Writers usually were monks who lived and worked in monasteries. The 11th through 13th centuries also marked the most productive period in Georgian literature. Shota Rustaveli (c. 1200) is Georgia's most famous writer. His masterpiece, "The Knight in the Tiger's Skin," continues to be celebrated as the greatest work of Georgian poetry. Its philosophical lessons have become the source of many Georgian proverbs.

Persian influence is evident in much literature of this era. Between the 11th and 13th centuries, some Georgian literature shows similarities with Persian epics of the time, as well as with literary works of Muslim culture. The late Middle Ages were a period of cultural decline in Georgia. The country lost its independence and was occupied by Mongol invaders from lands north of the Caucasus. During recent centuries, Georgia has produced a number of writers, but none of them have achieved Rustaveli's level of international recognition.

Music and Theater. Known for their warm hospitality and good spirits, Georgians enjoy lively songs and plays. Music, songs, and dances, now as in the past, are an important part of

Shota Rustaveli's poetic masterpiece, "The Knight in the Tiger's Skin," is considered the greatest work of Georgian poetry. The poet, Shota Rustaveli, lived in about 1200 A.D.

Georgian folk culture. People use every opportunity to spend time with family and friends. A traditional dinner called *supra*, provides a good excuse for singing and dancing. One Georgian folk dance is done by males, who dance on their toes without the assistance of special shoes. The Georgian State Dance Company is world famous for its performance of traditional dances. Georgia's folk music varies from region to region. Each ethnic group has its own folk traditions, thus providing the country with wonderful musical diversity. Theatrical plays are popular as well. The Rustaveli Theater in Tbilisi is internationally known for the quality of its plays, including those based on the works of William Shakespeare (staged in the Georgian language).

Traditions and Cuisine. Every culture has its traditions and customs. In Georgian society, traditions and customs are an important segment of people's lives. They also provide a people with vital links to the past. In a culture that places a high value on family life, it is not surprising that table customs and dining both play significant roles. Meals are family gatherings, often including friends and neighbors.

Georgians, like most other Europeans, eat holding the knife in the right hand and fork in the left. To foreigners, some Georgian table rituals may appear to be complicated. The custom of toasting provides one example. Wine is served with all meals except breakfast (during which tea or coffee are the preferred beverages). By tradition, however, it is proper to propose a toast before drinking wine—particularly during the evening meal. A toastmaster (*tamada*) leads the toasting—which may refer to health, weather, the country, individuals, or some humorous item. After each toast, everyone must drink his or her entire glass of wine. The tamada is usually a humorous person; it is his responsibility to ensure that there is a relaxed and pleasant atmosphere at the dining table. He follows strict traditions of toasting and cannot be interrupted by guests. If guests want to toast, they must seek permission from the tamada. Every speaker tries to be more original than the one before, but all try to emphasize love and friendship. Georgians usually do not toast when they drink beer. But when wine is on the table, toasts are almost required because a toast symbolizes power and beauty. Love of wine is understandable because Georgians have been raising grapes and making excellent wines for thousands of years. Some scholars even believe that people first began making wine in what is now the region of Georgia. This may help explain why Georgians are so proud of their vines and wines, and why they believe in the mystical power of wine.

By tradition, Georgians offer a toast before drinking wine. Georgians have been raising grapes and making excellent wines for millennia. At this banquet Mrs. Khaf Lasuria, who claimed to be at least 133 years old when this picture was taken in 1974, is a testament to the "mystical" powers of wine.

Georgian cuisine is quite similar to that found throughout much of the Mediterranean region and Southwest Asia. Meats include lamb, beef, chicken, pork, and fish. Eggplant, cucumbers, cabbage, and several types of beans are popular foods. Onions and garlic add zest to many dishes, as do a variety of spices and herbs used in Georgian cooking. A traditional evening meal might consist of soup, meat and potatoes, vegetables, bread, and several salads.

Recipes and ingredients can provide insights into food preferences and restrictions; knowing what people eat can indicate what crops and livestock they grow, or what they otherwise obtain from the environment; socially, elaborate,

1 kg medium eggplants
1/2 cup olive or vegetable oil
1 cup walnuts, shelled
1 tablespoon vinegar
2 tablespoons fresh cilantro, chopped
1 tablespoon fresh parsley, chopped
1 tablespoon fresh celery, chopped
1 tablespoon fresh basil, chopped
2-3 cloves garlic
1 onion chopped
1 teaspoon each ground red hot pepper, marigold,
    seeds of coriander, fenugreek
1/2 cup water
Salt & pepper to taste

Cut the eggplants in two lengthwise, salt them and an hour later wash and squeeze them out well. Saute garlic and onion in oil until tender. Add walnuts, stirring constantly, for one minute. Remove from stove and add herbs and spices. Heat vegetable oil in a skillet and fry the eggplants on both sides until browned. Grind the walnuts with the garlic. Stir in the spices and the chopped herbs, vinegar, and salt. Pour cold water little by little into walnut mixture until it is sour cream thick. Spread each half of the eggplants with the walnut mixture and fold them in two.

time-consuming recipes hint of a traditional role for women in the home; and complex dining suggests the existence of strong social bonds between family members and perhaps friends and neighbors.

Typical ingredients of Georgian cuisine are suggested in the popular recipe for fried eggplant with walnuts shown above.

Georgia, is a country of many cultures. Each ethnic group maintains many of its own cultural traditions, and the country does suffer from ethnic conflicts. From this diversity, over many millennia, a way of life that is distinctly "Georgian" has evolved.

Under Soviet control, agriculture was collectivized and people did not own or work their own land. The transition to a free market economy has been a difficult transition for many people to make.

CHAPTER

5

Government and Economy

Georgia's government and economy continue to falter as they struggle to overcome the legacy of former Soviet control and a host of domestic problems. During the seven decades of Soviet dominance, nearly all aspects of Georgia's economy were tightly planned and firmly controlled from Moscow. Even though Georgia's economy has been free of this influence for more than a decade, economic development has been a slow process. Immediately after achieving independence, Georgia's gross domestic product (the value of all goods and services produced in the country) dropped by nearly 80 percent. Although Georgia is now an independent state, government influence on the country's economy remains very much in evidence.

Government

Georgia's governmental structure is similar to that found today in many other former Soviet Republics. A primary feature is the dominant role played by a powerful head of state. During the Soviet era, Georgia's government and other political activities were under the firm grip of the Communist government. Moscow also controlled much of the country's economic activity.

After independence in 1991, the country held its first democratic, multiparty elections. A democratic government was organized and a president was elected as the country's leader. In 1995, a national referendum brought further change in the form of a new constitution. A peaceful presidential election and transition of government held the same year represented a milestone for Georgia's young democracy. Presidents are elected to a five-year term of office. Should a president no longer be able to serve, the chairman of the Parliament is the first in line successor.

Most former Soviet republics, including Georgia, have a unitary political system. Under this arrangement, the central government holds nearly all power. Local governments have little influence or importance. Nearly all political decisions are made by the government's executive branch (the president and his advisers) located in the national capital. Under this policy, most economic and other resources are directed toward the capital city—in Georgia, to Tbilisi. This leads to a great regional imbalance in development and human welfare. Capital cities, usually the country's largest and richest, become the centers of growth and prosperity. Meanwhile, the remainder of the country suffers from minimal attention, inadequate resources, and little development.

Modern Presidency. The democratic election of a president from candidates representing different political parties is a new experience in Georgia. In 1991, Zviad Gamsakhurdia became the country's first democratically elected president.

Under his leadership, democracy got off to a shaky start. Gamsakhurdia disappointed many Georgians because he adopted methods of government similar to those used by the Soviets. After only a year in office, he was overthrown by a violent coup, and the conflict rapidly escalated into a disruptive civil war. A military council, later formally named the State Council, took over the government.

This setback to democratic government proved to be temporary. The turbulent times ended when a former Soviet foreign minister and native Georgian, Edward Shevardnadze, became leader of the State Council. His reputation as a skilled politician and international diplomat was widely recognized and respected. He also had strong ties with governments in the West. This background played a major role in Shevardnadze's election to the presidency in 1995.

In Georgia, the president is the head of government and chief of state. He is also the supreme commander of the armed forces and presides over the National Security Council. The person holding this office is, by all measures, the most powerful person in the country. The annual military budget is determined and approved by the Parliament. Today, Georgian military forces number around 43,000 soldiers. Edward Shevardnadze's popularity among citizens after his first election did not fade. In 2000 he was elected to a second five-year term, receiving 80 percent of the votes. To most Georgians, Shevardnadze appeared to be the only politician with the stature and ability to bring peace to their troubled land, to restore a faltering legal system, and to fight against a rising tide of corruption. His determination to achieve these goals has met stern opposition from many individuals who in some way benefit from existing conditions. In fact, during his presidency, Shevardnadze has survived two assassination attempts.

During the mid-1990s, Shevardnadze organized a major attack against organized crime. This infuriated those who are involved in and profiting from Georgia's Mafia activity. Ironically, his inability to successfully gain control over rampant corruption has also cost him the support of many voters. In November 2001, angry demonstrators stormed the streets of Tbilisi to protest the president's inability to stop the criminal activity plaguing the nation.

Legislative and Judiciary Branches. Georgia's Parliament, or Supreme Council, is the country's highest political decision-making group. It is a unicameral body (a single legislative house, or chamber) composed of 235 elected deputies who serve four-year terms. They represent the country's three major and several minor political parties. The current ruling group is the Citizen's Union of Georgia, headed by Edward Shevardnadze (in the 2000 legislative election, its members received about 42 percent of the vote). The Parliament plays a major role in determining Georgia's domestic and foreign policy. It also oversees a number of other government responsibilities that are detailed in the country's constitution. A Supreme Court and Constitutional Court form the judicial branch of government. Judges are recommended by the president and approved by the Supreme Council.

Local and Regional Governments. Local and regional governments in Georgia are structured on four levels. Villages and towns represent the first level. Districts and regions form the next two levels of government. Finally, the fourth level is reserved for Georgia's two autonomous republics, Abkhazia and Ajaria. The president has the legal power to appoint the highest representatives for all levels of regional and local government. Abkhazia and Ajaria, however, are largely self-governed and can select their own leaders.

Abkhazia and Ajaria are autonomous republics, or semi-self-governing administrative subdivisions, within Georgia. The remainder of the country is divided into 10 regions (9 established regions and Tskhinvali, a region the status of which remains undetermined). Tbilisi, as the capital city,

Georgian women take part in the presidential elections in Tbilisi on April 9, 2000.

holds a special status equal to that of a region. The 10 regional governments are further divided into 65 districts, and approximately 60 district towns, 50 small towns, and 4,500 villages. Even the smallest units, the villages, are further divided into nearly 950 village councils. Local governments have some voice in local affairs such as taxes, economic development, education, medical care of citizens, and a number of other local services and concerns.

Foreign Affairs. Today, as in centuries past, Georgia's strategic geographic location and gateway function are important to its foreign policy. It must tread carefully as a Christian nation in a region increasingly dominated by Islamic militants. The international thirst for petroleum also casts a spotlight on Georgia. The country is in an oil-rich region (although its own petroleum resources are meager). It is considered to be a prime location to be crossed by one or more pipelines that would transport crude oil from fields near the Caspian Sea to Eastern Europe.

Georgia is a member of the United Nations. It is tied to the European community through membership in the Organization for Security and Co-operation in Europe (O.S.C.E.). Georgia also holds membership in the Commonwealth of Independent States (C.I.S.), a regional organization established among former Soviet republics after dissolution of the U.S.S.R. Relations between Georgia and the United States are very good, with increasing cooperation in humanitarian, economic, and political issues. Georgia's primary source of foreign irritation is its ongoing conflict with Russia over Abkhazia and neighboring Chechnya. For years, the Georgian government has accused Russia of helping rebels in Abkhazia (which wants to break away from Georgia). Meanwhile, Russia accuses Georgia of supporting Chechen rebels (who are attempting to break away from Russia). The normalization process between Georgia and Russia is slow, but in the early 21st century it seems to be improving.

Economy

More than 2000 years ago, ancient Greeks and others spoke of Georgia as being one of the world's richest kingdoms. Later, during its golden age of the 12th and 13th centuries, its people also prospered. During recent centuries, however, the country's economy has fallen on hard times.

Postindependence Economic Developments. A number of factors have influenced the Georgian economy since its independence from the U.S.S.R. in 1991. Unfortunately, most of them have had a negative impact. Ethnic conflicts in Abkhazia and South Ossetia have taken an enormous toll on the country's economy. Resources better spent on development have gone to support the military. Railroads, highways, and bridges have been destroyed. Hundreds of thousands of lives have been lost. Agriculture, industry, and services have been seriously disrupted by the turmoil.

Organized crime, attributed to a Georgian Mafia, has sapped many of the country's financial resources. Corruption seems to have reached its way into all aspects of Georgia's economy and government. During recent years, the public has become increasingly impatient over the government's inability to stop the widespread corruption.

Georgia also has been slow in making the transition from a centrally planned to free market economy. Under Soviet control, agriculture was collectivized and people did not own and work their own land. Industry also was government owned and controlled. There were very few incentives for hard work or individual initiative under the stifling Communist system. The transfer of land, industries, and businesses from government to private ownership is painstakingly difficult and time-consuming. Changing from a socialistic welfare state to an open, highly competitive, free market economy is also a very difficult transition for many people to make.

Finally, Georgia's relationship with Russia has changed. During its seven decades under Soviet dominance, Georgia played an important role in the U.S.S.R.'s economy. With its subtropical climate, it was able to provide a variety of warm weather crops to the some 250 million people living in colder lands north of the Caucasus. Warm weather and beautiful scenery combine to make Georgia one of the Soviet Union's most attractive tourist destinations. The Soviets also developed a number of industries in its republics south of the Caucasus. After the Soviet collapse, the centralized economy and market eroded as well. As yet, freer market policies and a democratic government have not been able to establish a solid foundation and infrastructure for economic growth.

Georgia has a variety of environmental conditions and natural resources. Much of the land is rugged, reducing arable (land that can be farmed) land to about 10 percent of its area. Pastures occupy another 25 percent of the country, much of it in rugged uplands. Another one-third of the country is covered by forests and woodlands. Georgia's land, resources, government, and people have combined to develop different sectors of the country's economy.

Tourism. Georgia is a beautiful country with breathtaking natural landscapes that combine with a rich cultural heritage, all within a relatively small and accessible area. A mild subtropical climate with warm winters and mild summers makes the Black Sea coast a year-round tourist attraction. Regular tourists and members of the Soviet Union's Communist Party flocked to the region. During the Soviet era, the coastal city of Sukhumi became one of the most popular tourist centers in the former U.S.S.R. The Caucasus Mountains offer spectacular scenery. They also have more pleasant weather than the lowlands during the summer months. With development, the mountains could be used by tourists for skiing, snowboarding, and other winter activities. Additionally, Georgia has much to offer tourists who are interested in traditional cultures, the arts and architecture, agriculture, and scenic rural landscapes.

During the latter half of the 20th century, millions of tourists (mainly from the Soviet Union) visited Georgia each year. Most were attracted to Black Sea coastal resorts. Many, however, came to see the region's agricultural landscapes, including its famous vineyards. Tourism, in fact, was the best-developed and most profitable branch of Georgia's economy.

Since its independence in 1991, however, tourism has plummeted and with it the tourist-based economy. Particularly damaging has been the ethnic violence and associated political turmoil. Secessionist-minded Abkhazia was the primary coastal tourist destination, particularly around its largest city,

Although civil strife has driven many foreign tourists to find alternate destinations for their wanderlust, tourism may still be Georgia's most important economic resource. A hike from the Caucasus Mountains to the coast of the Black Sea is a popular walk for hikers visiting Georgia.

Sukhumi. When civil war broke out, most tourists decided to choose more peaceful destinations. A decade of severe economic crisis also has affected tourism. Money simply has not been available—from either the government, domestic private investors, or foreign interests—to rebuild or further develop the crumbling tourist infrastructure (ranging from transportation facilities to lodging, dining, and recreational opportunities).

Tourism may be Georgia's single most important potential economic resource. To reach or surpass the level it enjoyed during the Soviet era, however, several things must happen. First, crime and ethnic violence must end and political stability must come to the country. Second, transportation facilities and routes have to be repaired and upgraded, and the countryside must be made safe for travelers. Third, attractive hotels and restaurants need to be renovated or built. Finally, the region must be "discovered" by foreign travelers and become known as a pleasant and attractive tourist destination. Fortunately, the Georgian government is beginning to restore once popular summer and winter resorts and to develop other resources attractive to the tourist economy.

Agriculture. Even though less than 10 percent of Georgia is well suited to crop production, the country has a strong agricultural tradition and economy. Approximately 40 percent of Georgia's labor force is engaged directly or indirectly in agriculture. And agriculture is responsible for almost a third of the country's gross domestic product. Georgian tea and its excellent wines are well known for their outstanding quality far beyond its borders. A mild, subtropical climate ranging from Mediterranean to continental to near desert makes it possible to raise a great variety of crops. Highlands are suited to livestock, and about 25 percent of the country's land is devoted to grazing.

During the Soviet era, Georgia was a major supplier of citrus and other fruits and vegetables raised mainly in the warm western lowlands. Today, it continues to provide subtropical and winter crops to the Russian market and beyond. Wine making is of particular importance. It is estimated that Georgia has some 150,000 acres of vineyards. The wine industry is concentrated in the valleys and lower slopes of eastern Georgia, although vineyards are scattered throughout the country. Wine making is one of the oldest

Tea is an important specialty crop and has been under cultivation for many years in Georgia. This photo of a large tea farm in Abkhazia was shot in 1950.

activities in the Georgian economy, tracing its origins well into the pre-Christian era. It is also the single largest contributor to the country's agricultural economy. Tea is another important specialty crop. It is grown mainly in the warm, humid lowlands of the western Colchis Lowland. Tobacco is another important specialty crop.

In the early 1990s, Georgia's civil conflicts severely disrupted agricultural activities. The country was plunged into a major food crisis, with production declining by more than one-third. As is true of other aspects of the economy, agriculture has great potential. First, however, peace and political stability must come to the region. And second, investments must be made in agricultural equipment and techniques to modernize farming and increase production.

Manufacturing. Industry contributes less than one-quarter of Georgia's annual economy. Before independence, most large industries were built and administered by the Soviets. Nearly 90 percent of all raw materials used by Georgia's industries were imported. Tbilisi, Kutaisi, and Rustai were and continue to be the major centers of manufacturing and commerce. This sector of the economy, however, lags far behind tourism and agriculture and is in great need of development. New factories, equipment, and management are all essential if Georgia is to develop this vital aspect of its economy.

Energy. Georgia has small amounts of coal, petroleum, and natural gas, as well as excellent hydroelectric potential. Yet it is unable to meet its growing demand for energy. The country is dependent upon costly imports of oil, natural gas, and electricity from Russia and other neighbors. Oil and natural gas come from Azerbaijan and Turkey; Russia and Turkmenistan provide electricity. The only significant domestic producers of energy are a number of hydroelectric power plants. Dams, reservoirs, and power stations are located on many mountain streams and also on the upper reaches of the Rioni and Mtkvari (Kura) rivers. It is estimated that as much as 40 percent of all electricity that is generated is lost because of poor equipment and maintenance during transmission. Additionally, Georgians are notorious for not paying their utility bills.

The failure to meet its energy needs with domestic production is one of Georgia's most severe economic

The inability to meet energy needs is a severe economic problem in Georgia. In December 1999 these children studied near a wood-burning stove in a home in the large city of Tbilisi. It was the only warm place in the room.

problems. Energy is essential to nearly all aspects of life, cultural growth, and economic development. Currently, Georgia must purchase a substantial part of its energy needs from foreign countries. This has strapped the country's economy with an enormous international debt.

Three energy-related developments offer some hope for the future. First is the recent discovery of offshore and onshore oil deposits bordering the Black Sea. Some forecasts suggest that Georgia may produce more oil than it consumes and even become a petroleum exporting country by 2005. Second, the country also is benefiting from the billions of dollars spent on leases, labor, and other necessary items by foreign oil producing companies.

The final oil-related windfall is related to oil and natural gas developments in the Caspian Basin, far to the east. Georgia's geographic location within a sensitive geopolitical region has made the country a logical route for the building of pipelines linking production and markets. Tremendous reserves of oil and natural gas have been discovered in and around the Caspian Sea. Only a single pipeline had connected oil-producing Azerbaijan, Turkmenistan, and Kazakhstan with outside markets. It links Caspian oil fields to southern Russia. But the route passes through a politically volatile area, including the Chechen Autonomous Republic that has been engaged in a heated civil conflict with Russia for nearly a decade. A new pipeline was completed in 1999 linking the Azerbaijan capitol Baku with the Georgian Black Sea port of Supsa. This new pipeline contributes much-needed foreign investments as well as profits from royalties. A second trans-Georgian pipeline is in the planning stage. This line would transport petroleum from Baku to a Black Sea port in northeastern Turkey. It would offer additional strength to the country's economy.

Transportation. Most of Georgia's transportation networks are old and poorly maintained. Improving transportation facilities is one of the government's priorities. The highway network is poorly developed by European standards. Much of it was developed and maintained by the Soviets. Civil war, political unrest, and Georgia's poor financial condition since independence have made it almost impossible for the country to devote attention to its decaying transportation facilities and routes.

Georgia is favored as a transportation crossroads because of its location. It sits astride north-south routes linking the Middle East and Russia, and east-west routes joining Europe and Asia. This geographical advantage attracts foreign investors and organizations that are willing to invest in highway, railroad, air, and seaport development. The seaport facilities at Poti and Batumi require improvement. Highways across the Caucasus, too, have to be improved. Currently, only three routes cross this huge barrier between Georgia and Russia.

Trade. In 2000, Georgia gained membership in the World Trade Organization (WTO). This was a major step toward future potential economic growth and stability. The country's economy continues to suffer, however, from a revenue-draining trade imbalance. The value of its exports amounts to less than half the cost of its imports. Georgia's most important trading partners are its neighbors, Turkey and Russia. Trade is increasing with the United States and other Western countries, as are American investments in the country's economy. Among the leading exports are agricultural products; manufactured goods, including machinery and textiles; chemicals; and minerals, including manganese (of which Georgia is one of the world's largest producers). Major imports include energy, grain and other foodstuffs, pharmaceuticals, machinery and parts, and transportation equipment.

Georgia's economy is heavily regionalized. Differences in climate, terrain, soils, ethnicity, and population combine to give different areas of the country certain advantages (or disadvantages) in developing the land and resources. It is a land in which history, too, has played a major role in giving a distinct "flavor" to various areas of the country.

During the traditional festival of "Tbilisoba" in the Georgian capital, residents of the city gather for a Sunday of dancing and singing in the streets, accompanied by traditional musical instruments, and also enjoy a variety of national dishes.

CHAPTER

6

People and Places

P eople give character and meaning to the places they occupy. A region may show the imprint of a certain type of farming, architecture, or religious belief. This imprint, the cultural landscape, is imposed both by people and their culture. Culture was discussed in detail in Chapter 4. Here, the focus is on Georgia's population and settlement, and the unique features of both.

Population and Settlement

The first Georgians occupied the region some 1.7 million years ago. This is the oldest record of ancestral humans living outside of Africa. Little is known about them, but we can assume that they hunted and gathered for survival and sought shelter in the region's many caves. Through time, Georgia's population grew. Early civilizations emerged, based on productive farming, and with them came early cities. A thousand years ago, Georgia was home to nearly six million people—a population greater than today. In fact, it was home to nearly as many people as lived in all of Europe at the time.

In 2002, Georgia's population is estimated to be between 4.5 and 5.8 million. The actual figure is not known because no census has been taken since the country's independence in 1991. Population density, for the country as a whole, is believed to be about 200 people per square mile (125 per square kilometer). This figure, as is true of most population density data, is somewhat misleading. In terms of settlement (where people live), nearly 90 percent of all Georgians live at an elevation of less than 3,300 feet (1,000 meters). The Georgian settlement pattern shows dense clusters of people living in productive and accessible lowland areas. Very few people inhabit the rugged, isolated mountain regions that cover nearly 80 percent of the country's total area. Clustering also occurs when the population distribution is viewed in terms of rural versus urban settlement. Slightly more than half of all Georgians live in cities (estimated 3.5 million). The remaining population is rural, scattered about the countryside, or living in Georgia's some 4,500 small towns.

Georgian life expectancy is lower than that of more developed West European countries, but by world standards it is quite high. On average, people live 73 years; men average a 69-year life span, and women 77. Amazingly, Georgia ranks among the world leaders, however, in the percentage of its population that lives to be more than 100 years of age. Scientists are unable to explain this phenomenon and the fact that most centenarians (a person living 100 or more years) live at high elevations in the Caucasus Mountains.

Georgia's population is stable to slightly declining.

Many factors help to explain this condition. First, as is true throughout Europe, Georgians are increasingly urban and educated, and many women have entered the workforce. Each of these factors contributes to smaller families. Second, ethnic conflicts have disrupted normal life patterns. They have resulted in an unknown number of deaths and many more people fleeing the country. Third, after Georgia's independence, many ethnic Russians returned to their own homeland. Fourth, because of its aging population, a high percentage of Georgians are beyond the normal age of reproduction. Finally, Georgia's poor economy and political turmoil discourage many people from wanting to begin a family.

Only 20 percent of Georgia's population is under 15 years of age, whereas 13 percent of its people are more than 65 years old. As is true throughout much of Europe, as well as in the United States and several other developed countries, this age balance poses many problems. As the population ages, there will be fewer and fewer young people in the workforce and an increasing number of people reaching retirement age. Another demographic (the statistical study of the human population) imbalance in Georgia is the number of men to women—there are only 91 males for each 100 females.

Georgia's Places

Three of Georgia's areas deserve special mention because they are unique—the autonomous republics of Ajara and Abkhazia, and the autonomous region of South Ossetia. Each of them is a semi-self-governing ethnic enclave, or small "island," inhabited by people whose history and culture are somewhat different from those of surrounding populations. Ajara and Abkhazia are located along the Black Sea in the western part of the country. Ajara borders Turkey and focuses upon the ancient port city of Batumi. Abkhazia, located in far northwestern Georgia, shares a border with Russia, and looks to its popular tourist destination, Sukhumi, as its leading center. South Ossetia is located in north central Georgia, tucked away in the southern slopes of the Caucasus.

Ajara. Ajara is smaller than Abkhazia, covering only about 1,120 square miles (2,900 square kilometers). Its population is remarkably diverse—more than 80 different ethnic groups live in this republic that is about the size of Rhode Island. The region is rich in history and culture. During ancient times Greek historians wrote about Kolkhida, western Georgia's historical kingdom. Present day Ajara was described as being a center of skilled stonecutting and metalwork.

As early as 1000 B.C. the region had a dense population. Nearby mountains were rich in minerals needed for the development of metallurgy, attracting people from all around the Black Sea and beyond. Seaports grew as Ajara's metals and manufactured goods were exported to the Mediterranean and kingdoms in Asia Minor. The region was also located on important routes linking the Mediterranean region and Southwest Asia with kingdoms to the north and East. Because of its strategic position, Ajara experienced many conquests and rulers throughout its history. Romans, Turks, Persians, various Georgian kingdoms, and Russians all fought for, and at times lay claim to, this small but important region. Finally, in 1878, Ajara was integrated with Georgia into the Russian Empire.

Ajara's ethnic and religious structure is the result of historical events. Even though Georgia is a predominantly Christian country, most of Ajara's population is Muslim. Ottoman Turks introduced the Islamic faith during their several centuries of rule over the region. During the troubled political times since Georgia achieved independence in the early 1990s, Ajara has managed to maintain a peaceful

Even though Georgia is a predominantly Christian country, the Autonomous Republic of Ajara's residents are largely Muslim. In December of 2001, 88-year-old Khusein Bakayev celebrated the Uraza-Bairam Muslim holiday with his family.

life without open ethnic conflict.

As is true elsewhere in Georgia, Ajara packs great diversity into a small land area. The environment changes from snow-clad mountain highlands to subtropical beaches in less than an hour's drive. Warm weather makes it possible to grow citrus and other fruits throughout the year. Tea plantations were established along Ajara's Black Sea coast during the 1880s. Mining continues to be important to the region. Copper deposits are mined in several locations, as are deposits of semiprecious stones and building materials.

Batumi has been Ajara's capital since 1921. This coastal city is the republic's largest community, and its cultural, educational, and industrial center. Its name comes from the Greek word *bathkos*, which means "deep." Batumi's geographic location and deep-water harbor are key factors in its role as a major seaport. Industrial goods, agricultural products, and oil are major exports. The city is at the western end of an oil pipeline from Azerbaijan through which millions of barrels of oil pass each year.

Abkhazia. Abkhazian people have a legend about how they came to their homeland. As the tale goes, when God was giving land to the world's people, Abkhazians were busy entertaining God's guests. After everybody got their land, God realized that he had missed the Abkhazians, so he decided to give them the small amount of land that remained. But only stones were left, so God had to use the stones to create a homeland for the Abkhazians. That is why, say Abkhazians, their land is not suited to cultivation, but its 3,300 square mile (8,545 square kilometers) landscape is full of natural beauty.

Settlers from ancient Greek city-states colonized the area of present day Abkhazia as early as the sixth century B.C. During its long history, Abkhazia was under foreign rule much of the time. A short period of independence was achieved in the eighth century A.D., but it was short-lived. It was integrated into the Georgian kingdom at the end of 10th century, and between the 10th and 19th centuries it changed rulers many times. In 1578, the Ottoman Turks gained control over Abkhazia and held it until 1810 when Russia gained control of the region. The republic's people reflect its history—ethnic Georgians are in the majority, but there are substantial numbers of Abkhazians, Russians, and several smaller ethnic minorities. Both Islam and Orthodox Christianity are widely practiced.

Abkhazia has a great variety of beautiful scenery. A short drive can take one from snow-capped mountain peaks, along sparking streams fed by glacial melt-water, to the balmy subtropical beaches of the Black Sea. Tourism has long been the region's major industry. Even during ancient times, Sukhumi's famous sulfur baths attracted health seekers from as far away as Rome. When the U.S.S.R. gained control of the region, Abkhazia became a major year-round destination for Soviet tourists. It was one of the few places in the country where citizens—many of whom were not permitted to leave the U.S.S.R. when it was under Communist control—could find warm winter and pleasant summer weather conditions, as well as a beach or the curing waters of a spa.

With its spectacular scenery, beaches and mineral baths, and fascinating cultural landscapes, Abkhazia has the potential to become a popular tourist destination. Unfortunately, the region's deep-seated ethnic tensions exploded into a civil war soon after the collapse of the Soviet Union. The Abkhazian Republic proclaimed its independence from Georgia in 1992, only a year after Georgia, itself, had achieved its independence. Georgia immediately sent troops into Abkhazia in an attempt to put down the secessionist movement. Thousands of people died in the fighting, and tens of thousands of refugees fled the republic. Much of the country was destroyed. A cease-fire was signed in 1994, but Abkhazia continued its policy of independence, including holding elections to choose its own leaders. The Georgian government denied the legality of Abkhazia's elections, and this complicated situation continues to the present day. Sporadic and

When the Abkazian Republic declared its independence from Georgia in 1992, Georgia sent troops into the republic and many refugees fled to avoid the bitter fighting. This woman welcomes back her grandchild to her home in Guria, Abkhazia.

terrorist activities continued into the early 21st century; the situation, although somewhat more stable, still is far from prewar normality. Even in peace time, it will still take years and millions of dollars to (re)develop the region's tourist economy.

South Ossetia. Ossetians are a non-Georgian ethnic group who live nestled away in the Caucasus. They are a fiercely independent people who—like so many groups in this culturally fractured region—have a strong sense of self-identity and a proud heritage. Although most Ossetians are Orthodox Christian, their language is related to Persian. Geographically and politically, Ossetians are divided by the Caucasus into two groups. Northern Ossetians live north of the Caucasus in Russia. South Ossetians live south of the range, occupying an area of approximately 1,500 square miles (2,430 square kilometers) located northwest of Tbilisi. Tskhinvali is their capital.

When the South Caucasus region was a part of the Soviet Union, the Ossetians enjoyed the status of autonomous region. When Georgia became independent in the early 1990s, however, its government attempted to fully integrate South Ossetia into the new republic. The independent South Ossetians rebelled and a civil war broke out. Nationalists in South Ossetia were demanding secession from Georgia. They wanted to join North Ossetia, which is part of Russia. Thousands of people lost their lives as a result of the civil conflict, and many thousands more fled the region as refugees. With the help of then Russian President Boris Yeltsin, a fragile peace was declared in 1992. Since then, despite occasional minor skirmishes, relations between the South Ossetians and the Georgian government have been stabilized. Today, the region is an integral part of the Georgian Republic.

A Tour of Georgia's Important Cities and Sights

Tbilisi. Geographers use the term primate city to describe an urban area that is a country's political, economic, and social "heart," as well as its largest city. With a population estimated to be more than 1.5 million, nearly one of every four Georgian's lives in this sprawling, cosmopolitan, capital. Tbilisi has been one of the most important settlements in the South Caucasus region from its very beginning in the fifth century.

Much of the city's importance is based on its strategic geographical location. Today, as in the past, it is a center of communication, transportation, and trade. Because of these roles, it also has long been an important military site. Located at the eastern end of Suram Pass in the valley of the Mtkvari (Kura) River, Tbilisi could control east-west travel, south of the Caucasus, between the Black and Caspian Seas. North-south travel across the towering Caucasus has always been difficult. Early Greek accounts tell of a single route that led northward from the present-day location of Tbilisi to cross the range into Russia. Russians improved this route, now called the Georgian Military Highway, nearly a century ago. Today, the route from Tbilisi to Russia crosses the Caucasus and winds through spectacular canyons and across several passes, including Jvari Pass at nearly 7,400 feet (2,256 meters). During winter months the highway is occasionally closed for short periods by heavy snowfall and avalanches.

Tbilisi is located on the banks of the Mtkvari River at the point where it breaks from the rugged canyons to the west. Although the city sprawls over a huge area, an excellent public transportation network of subways, busses, trolleys, and a tram provides easy access to all its districts. The city presents a mixture of old and new. Old districts have narrow passages winding by ancient buildings that date from the medieval period. Each year, the historical district is decorated for a celebration called *Tbilisoba*, which is held the last Sunday of October. October is important to Georgians. It is the month of harvest, including the picking of grapes from the vineyards, and a time to enjoy the fruits of one's labor. Earliest wines usually are ready to be tasted by the end of October. The annual first tasting is an almost sacred event for many Georgians who take great pride in the

Tbilisi has been one of the most important settlements in the South Caucasus since the 5th century. Today, the city presents a mixture of old and new, but all of Georgia's major educational and scientific institutions are located in this capital city.

long history and fine quality of their wines. In Tbilisi numerous events, including concerts and dances, take place during Tbilisoba. All of the country's regions are represented during the celebration, making it an ideal time to experience the richness of Georgian culture.

All of Georgia's major educational and scientific institutions are located in Tbilisi. The most important are the Tbilisi State University (since 1918) with over 20,000 students, the Academy of Science (1941), and the Georgian Academy of Art (1922). Theater is an important part of the city's cultural life, and Tbilisi is home to three long-established theaters that have earned widespread acclaim. Important religious structures include the sixth century Anchiskhat Basilica and Zion Cathedral. The Metekhi castle and church, built during the 13th century, is also an important historical landmark.

Telavi. The heart of Georgia's winemaking country is an hour's drive northeast of Tbilisi. Mile after mile of vineyards, and scattered wineries each steeped in rich tradition and pride, make this a unique and scenic rural landscape. Telavi is this region's center of population, education, economy, and culture. This city of about 20,000 has historical roots dating to its ancient role as capital of the Kingdom of Kakhetia. Many relicts from those feudal times are preserved.

Mtskheta. This city can be found by following the Mtkvari River a short distance west from Tbilisi. Mtskheta dates to the second millennium B.C., and in many ways it is Georgia's most important historical center. For a thousand years (c. 500 B.C.–500 A.D.), Mtskheta was the capital of the powerful Georgian Kingdom of Iberia (Kartli). Here appeared the first document written in the Georgian language and in its own alphabet. And it was in Mtskheta that Georgians adopted Christianity in the fourth century. Because of this important role, many of the city's important sites are related to Christianity. The city continues to be the administrative center of the Georgian Orthodox Church. Historical, religious architecture is preserved in the sixth century Jvari Monastery and 11th century Svetitskhoveli Cathedral. Religious art in the form of icons of the saints and details on the churches' portals can be seen in most of these buildings. Because of its historical importance, the entire city is included in the United Nation's list of World Cultural Heritage sites.

Gori. Continuing westward from Mtskheta, still following the winding valley of the Mtkvari River, travelers come to a city looked down upon by a huge, brooding fortress. The Goristsikhe fortress spreads over the hillside above the city of Gori. Georgian kings built this huge structure to protect east-west caravan routes that followed the Mtkvari River and crossed Saram Pass. Today, the city is the center of a small but important agricultural region.

Gori is the birthplace of Joseph Stalin, former leader of the Soviet Union. Stalin was a shoemaker's son but rose to become the ruthless supreme leader of the world's biggest country. His iron-fisted leadership spanned four decades, lasting from the 1920s to the early 1950s. Gori's most important cultural landmark is the Stalin Museum, which includes the small house where he was born and spent his childhood.

Kutaisi. This city can be reached by traveling westward from Gori and continuing along the twisting 110-mile highway that leads over the Suram Mountains from Tbilisi. This bustling city is home to more than 200,000 people, making it Georgia's second largest urban center. Although it is ancient, present-day Kutaisi is an industrial center with coal mining and the Kutaisi Automotive Works as its two main industries. The city is also the economic center of the large agricultural region to the west. The fertile, subtropical Colchis Lowland, located on the floodplain of the Rioni

The birthplace of the Russian revolutionary leader, Joseph V. Stalin (1879-1953) is in Gori, Georgia. Stalin ruled the Soviet Union from the 1920s to the early 1950s. This small house is part of the Stalin Museum that continues to draw visitors to Gori.

River, has been an important agricultural region for several thousand years. Historically, the city once ruled the ancient Georgian kingdom of Colchis. Its antiquity and importance are suggested by the ancient Greek legend of Jason and the Argonauts. The story describes a journey to "Imereti" (the kingdom) and "Kutaisi" (the city) in search of the Golden Fleece. Here, as is true of nearly all Georgian communities, history is writ in stone. The thousand-year-old Church of King Bagrat, for example, offers an example of medieval architecture. Sataplia National Park is near Kutaisi. Its numerous caves and preserved dinosaur tracks make the park a fascinating place to visit.

In 1990 Georgians demonstrated in the capital of Tbilisi on the first anniversary of a massacre of Georgian citizens by pro-Soviet militia in that city. Twenty people were killed in the massacre.

7

The Future of Georgia

G eographer Erhard Rostlund once stated, "The present is the fruit of the past and contains the seeds of the future." Rostlund could have been thinking about present-day Georgia when the statement was written nearly 50 years ago. It is necessary to look to Georgia's past before attempting to project its future.

The Past as a Prelude to the Future

The 20th century brought great political change to Georgia. At the dawn of the century, the country was a part of the Russian empire. Two decades into the century, its status changed to that of a republic within the new Union of Soviet Socialist Republics (U.S.S.R.). Finally, in 1991, it achieved independence. After a decade of independence, however, Georgia still faces many challenges. A lack of national unity, economic instability, and rampant corruption combine to make Georgia a difficult country to unify and to govern successfully.

Relations between Georgia's different ethnic groups were strained long before the country proclaimed its independence. Under firm Soviet rule, these antagonisms were not allowed to boil over into full-scale conflicts. Once Georgia became independent, however, the new government was unable to control the rising tide of ethnic separatism. In Abkhazia and North Ossetia, the fight for independence broke into open warfare in which thousands of lives were lost. Georgians feared that their country would become fragmented; Abkhazians and Ossetians feared that their culture would be lost if they were forced to share the same country with the numerically dominant ethnic Georgians. Whereas both conflicts were short-lived, cooperation and harmony among the country's different ethnic groups has not yet been achieved.

Internal and external political conflicts in the region have placed Georgia in a difficult political situation with its powerful Russian neighbor. Abkhazia and South Ossetia both sought to join the Russian republic, and Russia has fanned these flames of conflict in the region. During the past decade, Georgia has protested Russian intervention in its internal affairs on many occasions. Russia, meanwhile, has accused Georgia of giving sanctuary to Chechnyan rebels against whom they have been engaged in a lengthy armed conflict. Events such as these further complicate an already difficult relationship between the Georgians and Russians.

Economically, Georgia continues to face many problems. Shevardnadze's international reputation has been crucial in gaining financial aid (the United States, alone, has provided more than $800 million in aid since 1991), but the country's economy continues to stagnate. Two major problems stem from the country's relationship with the former Soviet Union. First, gaining its independence from the U.S.S.R., trade between Georgia and Russia experienced a huge drop, as did the number of Russian tourists visiting the Black Sea resorts. Second, Georgia is faced with the difficult task of restructuring its economy. Under the Communist system, nearly everything was state owned and controlled. Georgia is attempting to make the difficult transition to private ownership and control of property, industries, and businesses. The country's economy continues to struggle. In addition to the economic disruption caused by ethnic conflicts, warfare, and widespread corruption, inflation has greatly devalued Georgian currency (the lary). Salaries continue to be very low when compared with those in more developed countries. Since independence, the quality of life has declined for most Georgians, and they are becoming increasingly frustrated and impatient.

Political stability continues to elude the Georgians. In the last months of 2001, American newspaper headlines confirmed continuing conflicts: "Rebels threaten Georgia peace," "Villages attacked in breakaway region; 14 killed," and "Georgia head fires entire cabinet." Georgia faces corruption at all levels of government. Criminal elements also prey upon industries, businesses, and the general public. Most Georgians believe that corruption is the most severe threat facing their country. President Edward Shevardnadze has taken a strong stand against the crime and corruption, but the results of his efforts have disappointed many Georgians. Once celebrated as the person to lead Georgia to peace and prosperity in the 21st century, Shevardnadze is now rapidly losing popularity. In October 2001, thousands of Georgians took to the streets of Tbilisi in protest after police raided a popular television station, Rustavi 1, which had broadcast a program exposing corruption in government. Even though Shevardnadze fired his entire cabinet in response to the protests, the country was plunged into yet another political crisis, and many citizens asked for his resignation.

What Does the Future Hold?

Georgia is a country with enormous potential. It is a land of great natural beauty and variety, and it possesses a wealth of natural resources. Its mild, subtropical climate is ideal for growing specialty crops that can bring high prices in distant, mid-latitude, markets. Georgia's vineyards produce wines that could compete with the best French, Italian, and American vintage wines. If

International championships, such as this water skiing tournament held in the city of Poti on the Black Sea in 1998, bring sportsmen and tourists from many different countries to Georgia.

Georgia promoted itself and its products, Western consumers and investors would be aware of what the country has to offer.

Tourism may provide the key to Georgia's economic future. As a land of infinite natural, cultural, and historical variety—all within a relatively small and easily accessible area—the country has tremendous potential for year-round tourism. Summer and winter resorts can operate simultaneously, and within an hour's drive from one another. It is possible to spend an afternoon skiing the slopes of the Caucasus and then relax in the hot mineral bath of a Black Sea resort that evening. Also, as one of oldest Christian countries in the world, and with many well-preserved examples of religious architecture and art, Georgia could become a major center of tourism based on religion.

Georgia also can take advantage of its strategic location. Its position on a branch of the ancient Silk Road, long ago a major trade route between China and Europe, is attractive to foreign investors who are interested in reestablishing this ancient link between east and west. The country also provides a logical route for pipelines transporting oil and natural gas from the Caspian fields westward to the Black Sea and on to European markets.

If Georgia is to achieve prosperity, its people will have to bury many memories of the past and join together in concentrating on the future. As is true of other countries with a Communist past, Georgia's people are divided in terms of their views on development. Some cling to the past; they long for the "security" afforded by the socialist welfare state and are not yet ready to accept radical changes that are essential if the country is to develop. Others fully accept democracy, a free market economy, and the challenges of a competitive and rapidly changing way of life.

In summary, for Georgia to prosper, the economy, government, and society must become stable, and corruption has to be stopped at all levels. Many of the issues that Georgians face today will not disappear overnight. They are a legacy of the 20th century and before, and many will continue to dominate the way of life well into the future. But history has proven time and time again that Georgia's people are resilient; for centuries, they have faced adversity, but they have endured.

A decades-old Georgian saying can be applied to the country's future: "We are in ferment. We are not yet wine. We are still just *machari* (new wine)." For thousands of years, grapes produced by Georgia's soil, sun, and human toil have produced a mellow, mature, world-class wine. Georgia today is like machari. If Georgians can join together and use all available natural and human resources wisely and for the common good, their country will achieve a status comparable to that achieved by its excellent wines.

Facts at a Glance

Country name	Conventional: Georgia
	Local: Sak'art'velo
Location	Southwestern Asia, bordering the Black Sea, between Turkey and Russia, south of the Caucasus Mountains
Capital	Tbilisi
Area	26,911 sq mi (69,700 sq km)
Land boundaries	Total: 905 miles (1,461 km)
	Borders: Black Sea, 193 mi (310 km); Armenia, 102 mi (164 km); Azerbaijan, 200 mi (322 km); Russia 448 mi (723 km); Turkey 156 mi (252 km)
Climate	Warm and pleasant; Mediterranean subtropical on southwest Black Sea coast; humid subtropical, in the west central; and dry continental in the east; much of the country has a variety of highland climates, including permanent snow cover
Highest Point	Mt. Shkhara, 17,060 ft. (5,200 m)
Land use	Arable land: 9%
	Permanent crops: 4%
	Permanent pastures: 25%
	Forests and woodland: 34%
	Little economic activity: 28%
Natural hazards	Earthquakes, avalanches, floods
Environment—current issues	Air pollution, particularly in Rustavi; heavy pollution of Mtkvari River and the Black Sea; inadequate supplies of potable water; soil pollution from toxic chemicals
Population	4.9 million to 5.7 million
	(no census for more than a decade)
Life expectancy at birth	(2001 estimate)
	Total population: 73 years
	Male: 69 years
	Female: 77 years
Ethnic groups	Georgian, 70%; Armenian, 8%; Russian, 6%; Azeri, 6%; Ossetian, 3%; Abkhaz, 2%; other, 5%
Religions	Georgian Orthodox, 65%; Muslim, 11%; Armenian Apostolic, 8%; unknown, 6%
Languages	Georgian, 71% (official); Russian, 9%; Armenian, 7%; Azeri, 6%; other, 7% (Note: Abkhaz is the official language of the Autonomous Republic of Abkhazia)
Literacy	99%

Type of government	Republic
Head of State	President
Independence	9 April 1991 (from the former Soviet Union)
Administrative divisions	53 rayons, 9 cities, 2 autonomous republics
Flag description	Maroon field with small rectangle in upper hoist side corner; rectangle divided horizontally with black on top, white below
Currency	Lari
Labor force by occupation	Agriculture and forestry, 40% Services, 40% Industry and construction, 20%
Industries	Steel, aircraft, machine tools, electric locomotives, trucks, tractors, textiles, shoes, chemicals, wood products, tourism, wine
Primary imports	(c. $900 million, 2001 est.) Fuel, grain and other foods, machinery and parts, transportation equipment
Import partners	European Union, 22%; Russia, 19%; Turkey, 12%, United States, 12%
Primary exports	(c. $375 million, 2001 est.) Citrus fruit, tea, wine, other agricultural products; machinery, metals, chemicals, fuel re-exports, textiles
Export partners	Russia, 19%; Turkey, 16%; Azerbaijan, 8%; Armenia, 6%
Transportation	Highways: 21,000 mi (33,900 km) Railways: 983 mi (1,583 km) (does not include private lines) Airports: 31

1,700,0000	Evidence of ancestral humans (most ancient site outside of Africa)
50,000	Evidence early humans in the region
5,000	Neolithic (farming) peoples lived in Georgia
2100	Indo-Europeans invade Georgia
720	Nomadic people from the north of Caucasus invaded Georgia
600	Greek colonies appear on the east coast of the Black Sea
546–331	Period of Persian domination over the South Caucasus region
400	Formation of the Georgian Iberian Kingdom
66-65	Beginning of 400 years of Roman influence.
A.D.	
330	King Marian III's accepts Christianity as St. Nino Christianizes Georgia
655	Arab invasion of Georgia
813	Armenian prince Ashot I becomes first of the Bagrationi family to rule Georgia. This influenced Georgian rule for much of the next 1000 years.
1089–1125	King David IV "The Builder's" reign
1184–1213	Queen Tamar's reign
1236	Mongolian invasion of Georgia; occupation continues through 13th century
1315–1350	Brief period of consolidation and attempts to reunify Georgia
1386	Mongolians led by Timur (Tamerlane) invade
1453	Capture of Constantinople by the Ottoman Turks; Georgia soon falls under Turkish domination.
1400–1800	Period of conflicts for domination over Georgia between Persia, Ottoman Empire and Russia.
1556	Russia captured Astrakhan, which marked beginning in its attempts to spread domination south of the Caucasus.
1795	After Persian forces sacked Tbilisi, Herekle again sought protection from Christian Orthodox Russia.
1801	Beginning of annexation of Georgia by Russian, Czar Alexander I abolished the kingdom of Kartli in eastern Georgia.
Second part of the 19th century	Growing nationalism in Georgia against czarist autocracy.
Beginning of the 20th century	Marxists represent the strongest movement for national liberation.
1906-1917	Georgian revolutionaries became divided on Mensheviks and Bolsheviks, which represented a radical faction. This is a period of affirmation of native Georgian, Joseph Jugashvili (Stalin) as a leader of the Bolsheviks.

October 1917	Bolshevik Revolution and Communist take-over of Russia
1918	Georgia declared independence from Russia. Major European nations recognized Georgia's independence
1921	Zhordania, Menshevik leader, fled after Red Army invaded Georgia
1922–1936	Georgia is part of USSR's Transcausian Soviet Federated Socialist Republic
1936	Armenia, Azerbaijan, and Georgia achieved status of Autonomous Republics within USSR
1930s–1950s	Forced, but rapid urbanization of Georgia under Stalin's rule. Georgian nationalism mellowed during this period. In 1943 Georgian Orthodox Church was resorted.
1972	Edward Shevardnadze became first secretary of the Georgian Communist Party. In 1985, Shevardnadze would become minister of foreign affairs of the Soviet Union.
1978	Ethnic tensions rise when Abkhazian Autonomous Republic threatened succession, because of alleged restrictions from Tbilisi.
1989	Another rise of Georgian nationalism resulted with 20 people dead after clashes with Soviet troops in Tbilisi.
1990	Zviad Gamsakhurdia, former dissident, elected as Georgia's leader in first multi-party elections since 1921
April 1991	Parliament of Georgia adopted the Declaration of Independence.
Autumn 1991	Georgia's political situation deteriorated
1992	Coup d' état, Gamsakhurdia flees, Edward Shevarnadze returns to Georgia to head the Georgian State Council.
1992	International recognition of Georgia and the country was adopted in the United Nations as its 179th member.
1990s	Ethnic conflicts became reality in Georgia. Conflicts in South Ossetia and Abkhazia led to the further destabilization of the country. Yeltsin, Shevardnadze, and Ossetian representatives agreed to a ceasefire and regulation of the conflict in South Ossetia. In Abkhazia, after heavy battles, ceasefire was declared in 1993, but tensions remained strong through the entire decade.
1995	Edward Shevardnadze elected as president of Georgia
2000	Edward Shevardnadze re-elected to a second term as president

Glossary

area: A territory not necessarily unified (as opposed to region which implies similarity, or homogeneity); a vague reference to territory, such as "south of the Caucasus."

bora: Cold and often violent winter winds that sweep into western Georgia during winter months, drastically dropping temperatures and bringing misery to the region.

culture: The total way of life of a people, including their ideas, material things, beliefs, habits, social patterns, language, and all other traits.

cultural ecology: The ways in which a culture interacts with its physical environment, including its adaptation to, use of, and changes made in the environment.

ethnic(ity): A minority population, sharing a common sense of self-identity.

foehn: Winds that blow down mountain slopes, heating as they descend, and bringing warming conditions to lower elevations.

nation: The territory or area occupied by a nationality of peoples or a group having a strong sense of self-identity.

nation-state: A self-governed territory that also is a nation, or territory occupied primarily by one nationality of people.

primate city: A city that dominates a country's population, economy, cultural activity, and government.

Region(al): An area arbitrarily set apart from others by virtue of its having one or more similar characteristics; regions may be either physical (e.g., Mediterranean climate), cultural (e.g., the Christian realm), or historical (e.g., the Roman Empire).

state: Any governed territory, area, or region.

Transcaucasia: Russian term, adopted by the West, for the lands lying immediately south of the Caucasus Mountains. Because of its political connotation, Georgians and others in the region prefer "South Caucasus."

Central Intelligence Agency. *CIA—The World Factbook, Georgia.* *www.cia.gov/cia/publications/factbook* (current).

Curtis, Glenn E. (ed.). *Armenia, Azerbaijan, and Georgia: Country Studies.*

World Handbook Series, Library of Congress; Washington, D.C.: Superintendent of Documents, U.S. Government Printing Office, 1995.

Lang, David M. *The Georgians.* New York: Frederick A. Praeger Publishers,1966.

Suny, Ronald G. *The Making of the Georgian Nation.* Bloomington, IN: Indiana University Press, 1988.

Index

Index

Ossetians, 27, 44, 48, 51-52, 68-69, 81, 82, 86, 96
Ottoman Turks, 37, 39-40, 40, 41, 48, 51, 55, 82, 84

Parliament, 64, 65, 66
Pavlovich Beria, Lavrenti, 42-43
Persians, 34, 36, 39-40, 48, 55, 57, 82
Physical landscapes, 10, 13, 15-18, 20-23, 25-27, 70, 85
Place names, 10, 25-26, 31, 48
Population, 53, 79-81
Ports, 25, 77, 81, 84
Precipitation, 21, 22, 23, 27
Presidency, 64-67

Recreation, 25
Regional organizations, 68
Religion, 10, 34, 36-37, 38, 39, 40, 51, 52, 53-55, 57, 67, 82, 85, 87, 90-91, 98
Rioni River, 15, 18, 23, 31, 74, 91-92
Romans, 34-36, 48, 55, 82
Rural areas, 18, 80
Russia, 10, 12, 15, 17, 39, 40-41, 48, 50-51, 56, 68, 69, 72, 77, 82, 84, 87, 95, 96
Russians, 50-51, 81, 82, 85
Rustai, 74
Rustaveli, Shota, 57

Sakartvelo, 10, 31
Selchukid Turks, 37
Settlement pattern, 80
Shamil, 40
Shevardnadze, Edward, 43, 44, 65, 66, 96, 97
Shkhara, Mt., 17
Soil, 22, 27, 77
Sokhumi, 25
South Caucasus, 12
South Caucasus Mountains, 87
South Ossetians, 27, 44, 48, 51-52, 68-69, 81, 82, 86, 96

Soviet Union, 12, 26, 30, 41-43, 48, 51, 53, 63, 64, 69, 70, 72, 74, 85, 87, 95, 96-97
Stalin, Joseph, 41, 42-43, 91
Sukhumi, 32, 70, 71, 82, 85
Suram Mountains, 31, 91
Suram Pass, 18
Swans, 52

Tamar, Queen, 38
Tamerlane (Timur), 38, 48
Tbilisi, 18, 36, 37, 38, 41, 54, 56, 59, 64, 66-67, 74, 87-88, 90
Tbilisoba, 88, 90
Tea, 72, 73, 84
Telavi, 90
Theater, 58-59, 90
Tobacco, 73
Tourist industry, 27, 69, 70-72, 74, 82, 85, 86, 96, 98-99
Trade, 18, 25, 77, 84, 96
Transcaucasia, 12, 47
Transportation, 76-77, 88, 91
Turkey, 77

United Nations, 44, 68
United States, 68, 77, 96

Vakhtang Gorgaslan, King, 36
Vakhtang VI, King, 39
Vegetables, 72
Vegetation, 22-23, 70

Water features, 13, 15, 16, 17, 18, 20, 21, 23, 25-26, 27, 70, 74
Winds, 21, 25
Wines, 59, 70, 72-73, 88, 90, 97-98, 99
World Trade Organization (WTO), 77
World War I, 41
World War II, 43

Yeltsin, Boris, 44, 87

About the Author

ZORAN "ZOK" PAVLOVIĆ was born in Zagreb, Yugoslavia (now Croatia). He moved to the United States in 1999 and is pursuing his passion for learning about the world's people and places as a geography major at South Dakota State University in Brookings.

CHARLES F. "FRITZ" GRITZNER is Distinguished Professor of Geography at South Dakota State University. He is now in his fifth decade of college teaching and research. Much of his career work has focused on geographic education. Fritz has served as both president and executive director of the National Council for Geographic Education and has received the Council's George J. Miller Award for Distinguished Service.